ELEVEN CARDINALS SPEAK
ON MARRIAGE AND THE FAMILY

Eleven Cardinals Speak on Marriage and the Family

Essays from a Pastoral Viewpoint

Edited by
Winfried Aymans

Translated by
Michael J. Miller et al.

IGNATIUS PRESS   SAN FRANCISCO

Cover design by Roxanne Mei Lum

CONTENTS

Preface, by Winfried Aymans   vii

Carlo Cardinal Caffarra, Archbishop of Bologna
   Mercy and Conversion   I

Baselios Cardinal Cleemis, Major Archbishop-Catholicos of
the Syro-Malankara Catholic Church
   Marriage and Family: A Covenant with God in His Church;
   A Malankara Perspective on Marriage and Family   II

Paul Josef Cardinal Cordes, President Emeritus of the Pontifical
Council *Cor Unum*
   "Without Rupture or Discontinuity"   17

Dominik Cardinal Duka, O.P., Archbishop of Prague
   Reflections on the Family   39

Willem Jacobus Cardinal Eijk, Archbishop of Utrecht
   Can Divorced and Civilly Remarried Persons Receive Communion?   45

Joachim Cardinal Meisner, Archbishop Emeritus of Cologne
   Marriage Preparation—The Challenges of Today   55

John Cardinal Onaiyekan, Archbishop of Abuja (Nigeria)
   Marriage in Our Contemporary World: Pastoral Observations from
   an African Perspective   63

Antonio Maria Cardinal Rouco Varela, Archbishop Emeritus
of Madrid
   Witness to the Truth of the Gospel of the Family: An Urgent
   Pastoral Challenge for the Church to Set Out on the Journey of
   the Third Millennium   73

Camillo Cardinal Ruini, Vicar General Emeritus of His Holiness
for the Diocese of Rome
   The Gospel of the Family in the Secularized West   83

Robert Cardinal Sarah, Prefect of the Congregation for Divine
Worship and the Discipline of the Sacraments
  Marriage Preparation in a Secularized World   89

Jorge L. Cardinal Urosa Savino, Archbishop of Caracas
  Christian Marriage: The Reality and Pastoral Care   113

PREFACE

It is the heartfelt desire of Pope Francis that the Church reflect on the current situation of marriage and the family and to develop, to the extent possible, helpful recommendations for overcoming the difficulties. In order to underscore the importance of this topic, he first of all convoked two synods of bishops that are thematically interconnected but organized to include some different personnel, so as to create an opportunity for a wider public discussion over a longer period of time.

Of course it is not true that it has just now become evident how important it is—especially for the Church, too—to deal with the topic of marriage and family. We need only recall here the Second Vatican Council with its Pastoral Constitution, *Gaudium et spes* (articles 47–52), and also the Fifth Ordinary Synod of Bishops in 1980, which led to the great Post-Synodal Exhortation *Familiaris consortio* by Pope John Paul II, who meanwhile has been raised to the honors of the altars. This document can by all means be described as the Magna Carta of the Church's understanding of marriage and family in our time.

Yet since then the times have not stood still. In particular, in the so-called Western world, both the concept of marriage and the understanding of the family have been dissolving in an unprecedented way. Even in the twentieth century, there were strong efforts—at least on the Church's part—not to let the chasm between the ecclesiastical and the various secular arrangements of marriage and family become too deep. The two sets of arrangements have drifted apart, nonetheless, and the main starting point of that trend was the ever-increasing frequency of civil law divorces. By now, though, the very concepts of marriage and family are in many respects no longer unambiguous in society, and to this extent they have become dubious. Hence it is all the more necessary for the teaching of Jesus Christ not to come into question and for Church teaching, unabridged, to find its indubitable expression in our days as well.

The notions that prevail, on the one hand, in secular society and those that result, on the other hand, from the Church's faith have drifted apart, and, because of this, problematic situations and conflicts are increasing. These have become noticeable above all in pastoral care. Numerous publications by very highly qualified authors about theological principles and foundations have appeared even in recent days. This prompted the thought of enriching the relevant discussion with several essays that aim not so much to continue the scholarly debate as to consider practical questions mainly from a pastoral perspective.

Nevertheless, in order to lend greater weight to the contributions and also to create greater interest, cardinals of the Holy Roman Church were invited exclusively to write essays for the present book. Most of them gained their experience in their important responsibility as diocesan bishops of prominent local Churches, some in other significant ecclesiastical duties. All of them, however, became familiar with questions about marriage and family life through their priestly ministry. The authors were asked, not to enter into further systematic discussions, but to write in the form of an essay their own reflections about their personal experience and perspective. All the authors deserve our respect and thanks for the fact that they took the trouble to compose their essays within a short time, alongside their official duties.

The result stimulates reflections of an entirely different sort. The practical conclusions are sometimes based on more fundamental reflections of a philosophical or theological nature; others presuppose this foundation and follow simply from practical experiences. In keeping with the essay format of the contributions, it seemed appropriate for publication not to try to group the essays by topic for publication, but simply to arrange them in alphabetical order by the authors' names.

Now we will introduce the individual essays, while calling attention to the points emphasized in each.

Cardinal Cafarra, the archbishop of Bologna, addresses a topic that has become especially relevant recently, thanks to Pope Francis himself: "Mercy and Conversion". The author recognizes that without due carefulness, terms like "mercy" can easily be exploited. Therefore, he shows all sorts of things that must be included when we reflect on the divine and human dimensions of mercy.

The major archbishop-Catholicos of the Syro-Malankara Church of Trivandrum and currently the president of the Catholic Bishops'

Conference of India, *Cardinal Cleemis*, limits himself to one aspect of his topic—the mystery of sacramental marriage—in his short essay entitled "Marriage and Family: A Covenant with God in His Church".

If a priest recognizes that a married couple is living in an irregular or failed marital situation, he cares for the souls of the parties concerned and encourages them to participate in the life of the Church as much as possible. In marriage preparation courses, young people are instructed in the basic questions of the faith, the sacraments, and Church life. Premarital cohabitation is very rare. When a homosexual inclination of one of the partners in a married couple comes to light and is not corrected, then the "innocent" partner must be helped, even to the point of declaring the marriage invalid. In the Indian Christian tradition, marriage is regarded not only as a matter between the two partners, but as being embedded in society as a whole. Moreover, the author explains the nature of "arranged marriages". The most important catechesis is to make the wedding ceremony itself as solemn as possible. The bride and groom receive the sacrament—according to the tradition of the Eastern Churches—through the priest; they are not the ministers but the recipients of the sacrament. Furthermore, the author explains several symbols within the context of the liturgy, whereby prominent significance is assigned to the example of Christ's covenant with the Church.

Retired curial official *Cardinal Cordes* has already on earlier occasions taken part in discussions about marriage and family. Now, too, he takes a stand in a way that is as complete as it is clear. The title of his essay, "Without Rupture or Discontinuity", indicates his concerns. Central to it is the issue of the Church's doctrinal and practical way of dealing with the situation of divorced persons after they remarry civilly. The statements about the relevant discussions in the hall of Vatican Council II may give the reader much food for thought. The author deals harshly with the alleged paradigm shift conjured up recently in Germany by the head of the Pastoral Commission of the Bishops' Conference, in which the so-called signs of the time are declared by this bishop to be the source of the faith. With regard to pastoral questions, the author addresses the topic of spiritual communion in some detail. These reflections are also invaluable for another reason, if we consider that frequent sacramental Communion by the faithful is a modern phenomenon anyway.

The archbishop of Prague, *Cardinal Duka*, with his essay "Reflections on the Family", makes a contribution based on his special experience.

In his view, the family has been going through a serious crisis since the mid-nineteenth century. Under Communist rule, which he experienced, official atheism led to a destruction of anthropology, and the family was pilloried as an exploitative institution. In this respect, the first and foremost task in such a warped, post-Communist society is to make man comprehensible again as the image of God. Love, too, must be opened up again to a Christian interpretation, in which it must not be mistaken for a negation of freedom but, rather, understood as self-giving. This includes the Cross as well, which is a glorification, not of torture and killing, but, rather, of faithful love.

The archbishop of Utrecht, *Cardinal Eijk*, deals directly with the (rhetorical) question "Can Divorced and Civilly Remarried Persons Receive Communion?" The author starts from the premise that in many Western European countries a widespread abuse has long since made headway. In his view, the bishop is obliged to stand up for those clerics who have the courage to oppose this abuse. In terms of pastoral practice, he points out two aspects of the problem: First, he considers much more thorough instruction in the faith to be an indispensable preventive measure; when all is said and done, if there are still irremediable shortcomings, the couple should be dissuaded from marrying in the Church. Next, more attention must be given to pastoral care for married persons whose marriage has broken up; he, too, recommends so-called spiritual communion.

The archbishop emeritus of Cologne, *Cardinal Meisner*, speaks about "Marriage Preparation—The Challenges of Today". He thinks that the message of our faith is not entirely foreign to the yearnings of men today but that they experience the true values in secularized society as trivialized values. In order to confront these distortions, what is needed first is a long-term marriage preparation program with an "education for love". As part of this, the theme of marriage and sexual morality must also be brought back from its marginalized position. In short-term preparation for marriage, the doctrine proclaimed by Pope Saint John Paul II could assume a helpful place. Two topics are indispensable in this preparation: the connection between love and fertility, which is rooted in God's creative will, and the language of the body as an expression of marital love. Then there should be an explanation of the religious significance of sacramental marriage. With respect to the German situation, the author advocates a common framework for marriage preparation programs;

participation in one could in some cases be made a prerequisite for a Church wedding.

We owe pastoral reflections from an African perspective about "Marriage in Our Contemporary World" to the archbishop of Abuja (the Nigerian capital), *Cardinal Onaiyekan*. He has distinguished himself as a specialist, especially in biblical studies, in which he also took an advanced degree, and in the 1980s, John Paul II appointed him a member of the International Theological Commission. The author describes how the first reaction to the statements made in connection with the synod of bishops in 2014 was marked by great alarm even among non-Catholics. The Catholic Church had been perceived as a rock standing in the breakers, while the original universal Christian consensus about the fundamental unity and indissolubility of marriage had increasingly dissolved in recent decades. People asked whether the Catholic Church was moving now into the mainstream of secularism. What the author is able to report about the Church in the midst of African cultures is extremely interesting, as is the way in which Catholics are trying to cope pastorally with special problems such as polygamy, premarital sexual relations, and the importance of offspring. He does not deny that the problem of homosexuality exists in Africa, too, but people there are far from drawing the same conclusions from the presence of this phenomenon as those in the Western world do. What the author has to say at the conclusion about the duties of synods is so valuable that all the Synod Fathers should take these words to heart. I myself researched the synodal element in the Church's constitution for my habilitation thesis, and so I know whereof I speak.

The archbishop emeritus of Madrid, *Cardinal Rouco Varela*, contributes an essay on "Witness to the Truth of the Gospel of the Family" that is theologically as profound as it is comprehensive. For all the noise about the so-called culture of the superficial and the provisional, we should not jump to the conclusion that the search for the truth in God, Christ, and the teaching of the Church, including and especially with regard to sexuality, marriage, and family, is irrelevant to the younger generation. The confusion in many minds with regard to marriage and family starts with the denial of the natural law, which has had catastrophic consequences. The author emphatically defends the natural law, because in it marriage as a community formed between man and woman and the family that grows from it are still recognizable as realities founded in creation. His essay also makes it clear that these institutions precede all human authority—including that of the state— and hence are immune to any manipulative change. "Nothing is more existentially necessary or more historically urgent than to return to an acknowledgment of the natural law that founds, supports, and orders marriage, above and beyond any historical constellation of factors" (see p. 77). This order of creation in nature, however, contrasts with the inherited burden of original sin, and hardness of heart follows from it, along with the calamity of divorce. This is staunchly opposed by Christ, with his redemptive love and his call to his disciples to overcome their own hardheartedness: "Abide in my love" (Jn 15:9). Herein lies the chief task of pastoral care: accompanying and supporting people in the process of overcoming their own hardness of heart.

The retired long-time cardinal vicar of Rome, *Cardinal Ruini*, turns his attention expressly to the West in his essay, "The Gospel of the Family in the Secularized West". Despite the increase in problems concerning marriage and the family since Vatican Council II, particularly in the Western world, the cardinal thinks that the subsequent development of the Magisterium, especially by John Paul II, has laid an adequate foundation for the treatment of these topics that is required today. The author suggests addressing the problem about admitting the divorced and civilly remarried to Communion, at least in part, by a simplification of the annulment process. Especially important to him, nevertheless, is the question of whether the spouses had sufficient faith to contract a sacramental marriage. He correctly cites a similar question raised by Cardinal Ratzinger during his time as Prefect of the Congregation for the Doctrine of the Faith. In this connection, I take the liberty of referring the reader to my article entitled "Uniti nel nome di Dio" ["Joined in God's name"], which was published in the June 9–10, 2015, edition of *L'Osservatore Romano* (www.osservatoreromano.va).

The former archbishop of Conakry, Guinea, and current prefect of the Congregation for Divine Worship and the Discipline of the Sacraments, *Cardinal Sarah*, chose as his topic "Marriage Preparation in a Secularized World". The author starts from the premise that—especially in the Western world—the majority of young people who wish to marry are already cohabitating. He warns, however, against the erroneous conclusion that, in consequence, one must merely give these young people an understanding of the sacrament (since they have already experienced all the rest) in order to arrive at a fully Christian marriage. In these cases, what is needed, instead, is a fundamental *sanatio* of their understanding of love, so as to show what the Gospel understanding of marital love is. In this regard, the author takes as his guide a wise remark by Chesterton, with which he prefaces his reflections: "Take away the supernatural, and what remains is the unnatural" (see p. 89). True love needs grace. Since it cannot be just a matter of an intellectual process, the author advocates a thorough marriage catechumenate, in which the two realities—the natural institution of marriage and its sacramental dignity—are brought together into a unity. For this purpose, with considerable spiritual and practical empathy, he outlines a comprehensive program containing a wealth of suggestions and valuable considerations. It is worth pointing out here the author's opinion that the Western world needs evangelization, most particularly with regard to the body and sexuality, since sexuality taken for granted is no longer an expression of love but rather a form of narcissism for two. This is certainly also the point at which the opposition between what is routine in today's society and the Church's proclamation is most pronounced. Even in ancient times, many (for instance, Cyprian of Carthage) thought at first that a Christian marriage was not at all possible. And yet it is. *Exempla trahunt*: examples are attractive. It is necessary, however, to speak also about the Cross, because true love can be understood only in terms of it. As a third component of marriage preparation, the author mentions common prayer (for example, for forgiveness and in thanksgiving) and the sacraments. Sacramental marriage, finally, is for the married couple a path to holiness, to which all Christians are called, each in his own way. Marriage preparation means, therefore, leading persons to a radical Christian conversion that affects their entire lives.

The archbishop of Venezuela's capital, Caracas, *Cardinal Urosa Savino*, thanks Pope Francis for making the family a special topic of the Church—as Saint John Paul II did before him. His essay is entitled "Christian Marriage: The Reality and Pastoral Care". The author laments the fact that a secularizing tendency has crept into the Church, that sometimes every possible secondary aspect is discussed, but there is hardly any talk about the religious side of marriage. Therefore, he addresses certain topics explicitly, for instance, the institution, the sacramental nature, and the indissolubility of marriage, its necessity for the family and for society, as well as the exclusive partnership between a man and a woman. The realization of a Christian marriage, nevertheless, is opposed by societal tendencies—an increasingly aggressive secularism and a comfortable consumerism, which are popularized not least by the media. Within the Church, there is a lack of religious instruction. Admitting to Communion persons who have civilly remarried after divorce contradicts the whole doctrinal tradition of the Church. The Church must resist the pressure of the spirit of the world. People who are in an irregular situation should, however, participate in the liturgy. In an anti-religious world, we should stop trying to be "modern" and, instead, strive to contribute to the creation of an inspiring atmosphere, as many religious lay associations so marvelously do. The valuable lay movements for pastoral ministry to the family that have developed in Latin America must be promoted, both for marriage preparation and for the accompaniment of married couples (family gatherings, anniversaries, and so on).

A cordial word of thanks is due to many people. Very special thanks to my confrere and colleague Fr. Robert Dodaro, O.S.A. who, considering my status as a professor emeritus, offered to share his experience with the manifold technical questions involved in the present publication. These arose in particular because this book is to be published at the same time in four other languages (English, French, Italian, Spanish) besides the original German edition.

Next I thank all the publishing houses who participated and, with regard to the German edition, especially Mr. Manuel Herder, who agreed without hesitation to include the book in the collection of Herder Verlag. Mr. Björn Siller, a manager at the Rome branch of Herder, kindly took charge of publishing the volume.

I should thank also all the translators who dedicated themselves with great devotion to this task.

For his assistance in making many contacts and for his personal and practical suggestions, I thank Dr. Giancarlo Caronello and also my colleague in Munich, Fr. Stephan Haering, O.S.B.

Munich, on the Feast of the Apostle Saint James 2015
Winfried Aymans

Mercy and Conversion

Carlo Cardinal Caffarra

Dulcis est Dominus per mansuetudinem et rectus per veritatem.[1]

These reflections focus on the act in which God's mercy shines forth in its preeminent form: *the forgiveness of a sinner*. This is an act that Thomas Aquinas deems more divine than the act of creation itself,[2] an act of exclusively divine competence: "Who can forgive sins but God only?"[3]

I start with a saying of Jesus: "[T]here will be more joy in heaven over one sinner who repents than over ninety-nine righteous persons who need no repentance" (Lk 15:7).

1. Through his creation, God manifests his perfections. Creation was designed and willed in Christ and was ordered to the sharing of the human person in the divine filiation of the Word.[4]

The fulfillment of this divine Christocentric plan included the reality of sin. The refusal of man's free will to comply with God's design was not unforeseen in the divine plan. Before the foundation of the world and the beginning of time, God provided for all creation, the human person in the first place, in Christ the Redeemer of man by means of his sacrifice on the Cross. "He was destined before the foundation of the world but was made manifest at the end of the times for your sake" (1 Pet 1:20). And in a perfectly parallel passage: "[He] saved us and called us with a holy calling, not in virtue of our works but in virtue of his own

---

Carlo Cardinal Caffarra is the archbishop of Bologna and first president of the John Paul II Pontifical Institute for Studies on Marriage and Family.

[1] Saint Thomas Aquinas, *In Evangelium Beati Joannis Evangelistae Expositio* 8, l. 1, no. 6.
[2] Saint Thomas Aquinas, *Summa Theologiae* I-II, q. 113, a. 9.
[3] Lk 5:20-24.
[4] Eph 1:4-5; Col 1:16.

purpose and the grace which he gave us in Christ Jesus ages ago, and now has manifested through the appearing of our Savior Christ Jesus, who abolished death" (2 Tim 1:9–10).

The eternal divine plan and human chronology cross paths when the Savior appears who conquers death. The eternal plan is then manifested within history in the face of a God who is rich in mercy.

The apostolic catechesis is unequivocal in this regard. The death of Jesus for the remission of our sins was no accident brought about by merely human factors: it had to happen. It was God's plan.

While creating, he could have decided to reveal his wisdom or his omnipotence above all else. Instead, he decided to reveal his surpassing mercy, to reveal himself as the God who is rich in mercy.

In the converted and forgiven sinner, therefore, God sees the full realization of his creative plan, and hence he rejoices over this outcome more than in contemplating the just man. The act of mercy that forgives is the summit of creation, since the latter was designed "to the praise of his glorious grace which he freely bestowed on us in the Beloved. In him we have redemption through his blood" (Eph 1:6–7).

"I read that He made man and then found rest in one whose sins He would remit."[5]

The thought of the great Bishop of Milan is profound. When God creates, the thing about himself that he wills to express as his ultimate and complete perfection is mercy. Now he can rest; he has nothing else to reveal: he has created a being whom he can forgive. The Redeemer is not a remedy for an accident that happened to the edifice of creation but, rather, the very end of creation. Each of us can say again with Saint Ambrose, "I will not glory because I am free of sins, but because sins have been forgiven me."[6]

2. The efficacy of a medicine is measured by the seriousness of the illness. Thomas says that the justification of the sinner is a divine act greater than the eternal justification of a just man, inasmuch as the distance in the first

---

[5] Saint Ambrose, *The Six Days of Creation*, homily 9, 10, 76, in *Saint Ambrose: Hexameron, Paradise, and Cain and Abel*, trans. John J. Savage, The Fathers of the Church 42 (New York: Fathers of the Church, 1961), 282.

[6] Saint Ambrose, *Jacob and the Happy Life*, 1, 6, 21, in *Saint Ambrose, Seven Exegetical Works*, trans. Michael P. McHugh (Washington, D.C.: Catholic University of America Press, 1972), 133.

case between the point of departure and the point of arrival (from sin to justice) is greater than in the second case (from the state of grace to eternal glory).[7] In order to have some understanding "of the glory of his grace", it is necessary, therefore, to grasp "what a great burden sin is".[8]

Sin is an act of the person. In his act and by means of an act of his free will, a person becomes who he is. The Fathers of the Church used to say that through his choices a person generates himself. If I think of a triangle, I do not become a triangle. But if I commit a robbery, I become a thief. This relation between person and act can occur for good and for evil. Let us consider the second hypothesis.

In describing the famous "night of the Unnamed", a scene from his novel *I promessi sposi*, Alessandro Manzoni presents the character of the Unnamed, a feared criminal who examines his past life. "From one bloody deed to another, from one act of villainy to the next.... They were all his, they were he ... the horror of this thought grew to the point of despair."[9] "*They were he*": the man and his acts. In thinking about free choices, one can speak about the self-creation of the human person.

It is logical that the Unnamed should think of suicide. Moral evil is something that has no reason to exist, something that should not be. But the cancellation thereof could occur only through the death of the one who committed the evil, provided, however, that it was the total death of the man, in other words, that it extended also to the deep source from which the evil decision was made: the "I", the person endowed with free will. But men, basically, have never believed that death had such a destructive force, at least from Plato on.

In committing moral evil, man imprisons himself. There is no way out. "All the perfumes of Arabia will not sweeten this little hand."[10] This was the hand that killed an innocent man.

But that is not all. Even before his own free acts, a human person is born in a state of sin, of enmity with God. This is what the Church's faith calls *original sin*. We have no responsibility for it. It is a congenital condition. In what does it consist? In the fact that everyone is born, not

[7] Saint Thomas Aquinas, *Summa Theologiae* I-II, q. 113, a. 9.
[8] Saint Anselm, *Cur Deus homo* 1, 21; cited in English from *Why God Became Man*, trans. Joseph M. Colleran (Albany, N.Y.: Magi Books, 1969), 108ff.
[9] Alessandro Manzoni, *I promessi sposi*, chap. 21.
[10] William Shakespeare, *Macbeth*, act 5, scene 1.

in Christ, but rather in Adam. Man was willed by God in the image of his only begotten Son, but he appears in his sight from the moment of his conception and even before any free choice of his own as deformed and fallen from the Image. Putting us in a position where ... As for God, he says: "You are not as you ought to be; you do not bear the image of my only begotten Son according to my design and will for you. You bear the distorted image of Adam."

This is why God, if he wishes to meet man, cannot do so in a neutral way, but only *mercifully*. The encounter—excluding the death of the sinner—must have within it enough strength to restore the person to his full justice, to annul those decisions by which the human person has disfigured himself. It must descend to the very core of the person, to what makes him say "I". This is the force that "is described as mercy". "And in man's history this revelation of love and mercy has taken a form and a name: that of Jesus Christ."[11]

3. Now we seek to tell about the encounter between God's mercy in Christ and man's moral misery. The *divine dimension* of this encounter is called *forgiveness*; the *human dimension* is called *conversion*. Forgiveness and conversion are two dimensions of the same event: there is no such thing as one without the other.

Before proceeding, however, one premise is necessary without which everything we say would be a house of cards. And this premise is made up of a "twofold postulate of its own, arising from its fundamental nature: first, that the 'Absolute' is free ... and second, that the 'Absolute' has a sovereign ability, out of its own freedom, to create and send forth finite but genuinely free beings ... in such a way that, without vitiating the infinite nature of God's freedom, a genuine opposition of freedoms can come about."[12] Scripture talks about a Pact, a Covenant, a Wedding between the two. These images decisively authenticate the fact that one stands before the other in respective freedom.

But the relation between finite freedom and divine freedom is not the same as the relation between finite freedom and a created object/subject. And this is true in two respects. The more my choice is moved by divine

---

[11] Saint John Paul II, encyclical letter *Redemptor hominis* (March 4, 1979), 9; cf. Pope Francis, *Misericordiae Vultus: Bull of Indiction of the Extraordinary Jubilee of Mercy* (April 11, 2015), 1.

[12] Hans Urs von Balthasar, *Theo-Drama: Theological Dramatic Theory*, vol. 2, *Dramatis Personae: Man in God*, trans. Graham Harrison (San Francisco: Ignatius Press, 1990), 190.

freedom, the more it is my own: this is the experience and the teaching of all the great Christian mystics. The second respect: as we examine in greater depth the opposition between the two freedoms, an abyss yawns in front of us between God's holiness and the loss of finite freedom that has fallen into sin, a loss from which one can be drawn out only if God's holy freedom turns to that finite freedom (= prevenient grace) in order to save it (cf. Augustine, Pascal).

This is the "stage" on which the drama is played out: the encounter of Mercy with misery, of the God who forgives because he is holy and man who converts because he is a sinner. We can outline the plot of this dramatic action, even though every forgiveness-conversion has its own story.

God is the one who took the initiative to reconcile us to himself in Jesus, who died on the Cross. Man is not the master of this initiative. But at the same time, God's initiative goes to the roots of man's moral misery and to the core of the "I"; otherwise, it would not truly heal. The New Covenant implies a new heart,[13] and every divine action is such that anything greater of its kind is unimaginable. The measure of the minimum essential is not God's measure. And, indeed, Scripture describes this action of Mercy using rather strong terms that cannot be minimized: re-generation; new creation.

Yet all this would simply be false if the absolutely free initiative of God in Christ *did not set in motion* the finite freedom of man. This is required both by the very nature of the human person and also by the relation that God intends to reestablish in Christ.

It is an essential characteristic of the human person to be in possession of himself (*sui juris*) by means of his free will. This is the principle of his own actions by virtue of his freedom and the mastery that he has over them. If forgiveness does not change the direction of his freedom, and he does not convert, we cannot truly say that a man has been forgiven.

The very nature of the relation that God wishes to reestablish in Christ is what requires the cooperation of the finite freedom. It is a Covenant relation; it is a Wedding; it is Friendship: none of these relationships can be formed without the freedom of both *partners*.

The Love that forgives has appeared, and it has stopped at the door of every human heart, waiting for someone to say to him: "Yes, come in."

---

[13] Jer 31:31-34.

On this invitation depends the highest revelation of the Mystery of God: the forgiveness of the sinner.

What human acts bring into being the person's cooperation? Two, fundamentally. Recognition of one's own condition of moral misery, one's own sin: "What I did is not right." This is the *repentance* that is expressed in *confession*. The consequence of this—the second act—is the decision not to do in the future what we acknowledge to be wrong: the *resolution*.

But although these are the two acts that mark the turning point, the change of course, the journey on the new course requires an ongoing attitude—in ethical terms, the continual exercise of the virtue of repentance. "The second reason why repentance must be perpetual is that every sin is like a wound; and although a wound heals over, the scar, the sign, the imprint [τυπος] of the sin remains."[14]

Conversion is an event and a permanent attitude. It is an event consisting of the *act* of repentance-confession-resolution; it is an attitude, a permanent condition, since the justice granted by Mercy seeks to enter into every fiber of the person. And this can happen only gradually.

The fruit of the encounter of Mercy with misery, of forgiveness with conversion, is the restored ability to produce fruits of justice, to perform good deeds. "God ... condemned sin in the flesh, in order that the just requirement of the law might be fulfilled in us, who walk not according to the flesh but according to the Spirit" (Rom 8:34). Note: the principle of fulfilling what the Law commands is not the Law but the Holy Spirit, and for this reason Thomas would conclude that the New Law is the grace itself of the Holy Spirit.[15]

This marvelous work of Mercy is what encounters misery; God's holiness meets man's sin. The encounter has a divine name: *the forgiveness of sins*; it has a human name: *the conversion of human freedom*.

4. There are mistaken stories about this encounter, performances of this divine-human drama that ring false. Mistaken and false because they do not relate what in reality occurs. And this can happen in two basic ways: mercy without conversion; conversion without mercy.

---

[14] Irénée Hausherr, *Penthos: La dottrina della compunzione nell'Oriente cristiano* (Bresseo di Teolo: Abbazia di Praglia Edizioni, 2013), 36.

[15] Saint Thomas Aquinas, *Summa Theologiae* I-II, q. 106, a. 1.

A. *Mercy without conversion.* This is the proclamation of a (supposed) mercy of God that is made without denouncing the sin of man and the sin of the world. It was no accident that the apostolic catechesis fixed forever in the memory of the Church the preaching of John the Baptist, as a voice that must never cease to reecho. Truth is held prisoner in injustice[16] and must be set free. In other words: it must be said that man must convert, and from what *actions* and attitudes, that is, *vices* he must turn away.

The Holiness of God is merciful; the Mercy of God is holy and sanctifying. "We must attribute to God positive qualities, like justice and mercy. For us these are two different qualities. A man can possess one of them without possessing the other. In God there is no plurality of qualities. His being is simple. Only we see the light refracted in the rainbow. This means: justice and mercy in God are not different qualities. We, however, cannot imagine the identity of these two qualities."[17]

Mercy without (any requirement for) conversion is not divine mercy. It is the mistaken pity of an incompetent and/or weak physician who contents himself with bandaging wounds without treating them.

B. *Conversion without mercy.* This is the Pelagian poison that kills the Christian proposition by reducing it to a moral code or exhortation.

Even pagan wisdom in its most exalted moments had in fact realized the necessity of conversion to the good. But they saw the goal and not the road leading to it; they did not discover the source that gives the strength to travel it. Augustine was the great instructor in this regard.[18]

But today in the West we find ourselves in a spiritual situation, a "spirit of the age" that has trivialized and emptied of its proper meaning the drama of the Mercy ↔ misery, forgiveness ↔ conversion encounter. It has turned the drama into a farce.

Proclaiming the Gospel of mercy and conversion, while ignoring this cultural fact, is like sowing seed on a pavement. It may please those who

---

[16] Rom 1:18.

[17] Saint John Paul II, private conversation with Prof. Robert Spaemann, cited in Robert Spaemann, *Dio e il mondo* (Siena: Cantagalli, 2014), 261.

[18] Cf., for example, Saint Augustine, *In Iohannis evangelium tractatus* 2, 16: "Do not let go of the wood on which you can cross the sea", in: *The Works of Saint Augustine, A Translation for the 21st Century*, vol. 3/12, *Homilies on the Gospel of John 1–40*, trans. Edmund Hill, O.P. (New York: New City Press, 2009), 67.

hear it, but it does not change hearts. It may reap consensus and applause, but it leaves the person as it found him. I think that this matter is of such great importance that it deserves a moment of separate reflection.

5. The proclamation of Mercy ↔ forgiveness can latch on to only one thing in those who listen to it: *the awareness of being sinners.* In this sense, Kierkegaard is correct when he writes that we are bound to the Christian message to the extent that we are aware of being sinners.

This awareness implies a deep conviction that in general there are such things as an erring life and a just life, such things as good and evil that precede and judge our free choices. There is at least a confused perception that the judgment of one's own conscience is rooted in an interior light that shines in the depths of the soul, to the point of entering into the very make-up of personal being: the natural moral law.

If this point of connection is missing, the proclamation of Mercy may even still be applauded, out of the conviction that this proclamation does not really concern me, since I have no need of conversion.

This can occur for two reasons. One is the condition of the "hardened heart" mentioned in Scripture. But this is not the most serious reason. The most serious reason is a theoretical and practical experience of *unfounded* freedom, which finds in itself its reason for being, without any further judicial authority. It is a freedom *from* the truth about man. This is a tragic condition. The Cross of Christ, as the supreme revelation of Mercy, is emptied of meaning,[19] since all talk about mercy means approval of what I am doing.

The distinction between subjective accountability and objective disorder, between "not being guilty" and "acting righteously", no longer has meaning. It is no longer conceivable, since right action has no foundation on a reality independent of individual subjectivity or the consensus of a majority in society. Accepting a homosexual means, in this context, recognizing the moral rectitude of homosexual behavior. To give one example.

In this context, the proclamation of Mercy means: "Accept me as I am and as I act, without speaking to me about conversion, since I have no need of it." With that we have arrived at the complete distortion of the Church's proclamation.

[19] 1 Cor 1:17.

6. I would like now to illustrate the whole preceding reflection by applying it to the question of admitting, even if only on certain conditions, divorced and remarried persons to the Eucharist. Not because it is the central problem of the next synod: at least I hope it is not.

The proclamation of Mercy ↔ conversion to these persons is the proclamation of God's offer of forgiveness and, therefore, of the requirement of conversion. Conversion from what? From the condition that objectively contradicts the good of indissolubility granted by Jesus. A contradiction that on the practical level is adultery.

As I have already said, conversion originally means a value judgment: "I have sinned; I am in a state of adultery"; it means a decision: "I will give up this condition" (judgment + decision = repentance).

"Give up" implies physical separation from the putative spouse, since only in that way will the adulterous habit be broken.[20]

There may of course be objective circumstances that morally impede physical separation, such as, for example, the right of any children who may have been born [of the second union] to an upbringing; serious health conditions of one spouse; the risk that the other spouse may fall into serious poverty. The hypothesis is found throughout the ethical-pastoral history of the Church,[21] and the response is unanimous: Give up the way of living out one's own sexuality that is contrary to Jesus' words by making use of the means of natural and supernatural prudence.

What is the basis for this common response, which is repeated by almost all the Doctors of the Church and theologians? It is based on the power of the Mercy of God, who forgives all sin—who, in other words, moves freedom toward the good, whatever a person's situation may be. "With God nothing will be impossible" (Lk 1:37).

What is implied when someone denies the truth of the preceding response? Either a person is asserting that *the condition* of adultery is not permanent, and then he does not see the meaning of the indissolubility of the sacrament of marriage. Or else he is asserting that it is impossible for man to convert, to live in chastity, and then "the Mercy of God is curtailed".

The fundamental question is: Which of these two is for "the greater glory of God", who is rich in mercy?

---

[20] See the propositions condemned by Pope Innocent XI, *Propositiones LXV damnatae in Dec. S. Officii 2 Mart. 1679*, nos. 61, 62, 63 = DS 2161–2163.

[21] See, for example, Saint Alphonsus de Liguori, *Theologia Moralis* 6, 4, 1, no. 455.

I conclude with a marvelous passage from Thomas taken from the *reportatio* of his Commentary on John 8:11.

> Finally, Jesus cautions her when he says, *Go, and do not sin again.* There were two things in that woman: her nature and her sin. Our Lord could have condemned both. For example, he could have condemned her nature if he had ordered them to stone her, and he could have condemned her sin if he had not forgiven her. He was also able to absolve each. For example, if he had given her license to sin, saying: "Go, live as you wish, and put your hope in my freeing you. No matter how much you sin, I will free you even from Gehenna and from the tortures of hell." But our Lord does not love sin, and does not favor wrongdoing, and so he condemned her sin but not her nature, saying, *Go, and do not sin again.* We see here how kind our Lord is because of his gentleness, and how just he is because of his truth.[22]

---

[22] Saint Thomas Aquinas, *Commentary on the Gospel of St. John*, pt. 2, chaps. 8–21, trans. Fabian R. Larcher, O.P. (1980; Albany: Magi Books, 1988), 105.

Marriage and Family: A Covenant with God in His Church

A Malankara Perspective on Marriage and Family

Baselios Cardinal Cleemis

Elevating the holy mysteries during the Holy Qurbono (Eucharist) according to the Syro-Malankara Rite, the celebrant loudly proclaims: "Holy mysteries to the holy people." The faithful respond to the proclamation: "There is none holy but the Holy Father, Son, and the Holy Spirit, who is one God forever and ever. Amen." As we reflect on the basic constitutive element of the Church and society, that is, the family, the very first thought that comes to my mind is that we are reflecting on a divine mystery that is entrusted to human participation. In this brief article, I am trying to explain only one aspect of the sacrament of matrimony, namely, the mystery aspect. It is a covenant rather than a humanly arranged agreement between two persons. Therefore, the sacrament of matrimony presupposes certain elements as natural conditions and the continuity of those conditions for a stable Christian family life.

The term "Malankara" represents the Saint Thomas Syrian Christian communities of India who have adopted the Syrian Antiochene liturgical tradition. The Saint Thomas Christian communities are divided into various groups belonging to Catholic and non-Catholic folds. The family as well as married life in this community are very much shaped by the Eastern Catholic teaching on the sacrament of matrimony and are influenced by the Indian scenario of a "mosaic of cultures" and "a land of religions".

I speak from the context of the Syro-Malankara Catholic Church (hereafter SMCC) when I say that the close pastoral care of the shepherds,

Baselios Cardinal Cleemis is the major archbishop-Catholicos of the Syro-Malankara Catholic Church and president of the Catholic Bishops' Conference of India.

who seek for the lost and abandoned sheep, shows the loving motherly heart of the Church. An effective catechism on marriage and family contributes to the further strengthening of family life. The SMCC custom of having a daily evening gathering of the family for regular Bible reading, hymns, canonical prayers of the hours, and rosary is a strong factor that enriches and sustains the Christian spirit of the family. The role of some of the pious associations active in the SMCC is also to be gratefully acknowledged. Once a pastor becomes aware that a particular family in an irregular marital situation needs pastoral support, he tries to understand them, clarifies for them the actual state of their union in the eyes of the Church, and invites and encourages them to attend the spiritual services in the Church and to participate actively in the social programs of the parish. He offers the possibility of baptizing their children, while he also seeks to regularize their union and visits and prays with them in their residence. Their children are offered full participation in all the spiritual services of the Church. In some cases, even if regularization of the parents' union is impossible, we try to channel God's love for them and make them feel that love. Some cases have been noted in which, for the sake of the children, the man and woman decide to live together in the same house but refrain from sexual activity.

We employ a similar pastoral approach toward those who live as separated spouses or who have divorced, those whose marriage has failed as well as those who have sought to marry outside the Church. While seeking a helpful solution for their problems within the legal/sacramental possibilities, the pastor encourages them to remain assured of God's love for them while also keeping them involved in the social activities of the parish. They are thereby helped to feel the Church's love and need for them. We leave the door open for them and encourage the children of such parents to participate in all of the Church's spiritual services.

The young people who approach the Church for marriage are made to undergo an intensive course on the essentials of the Catholic faith, sacraments, and life in the Church. Specially prepared guide books and the services of nuns or other trained persons assist in the preparation of young people for marriage. At present the SMCC does not experience the problem of heavy secularization among its youth. Pastors also meet them and speak with them regularly.

Cohabitation prior to sacramental marriage is very rare and exceptional among the members of the SMCC. This irregular type of union is not at all approved of by Indian society. When such a case arises, the candidates are kindly encouraged to repent, and they are prepared for genuine sacramental confession and for the sacramental celebration of matrimony at the earliest possible time.

The problem of a marriage in which one of the partners suffers from same-sex attraction must be dealt with through the motherly heart of the Church. If it is proven that the individual concerned entered into the marriage while conscious of an erroneous disposition and is unwilling to correct his disposition, even with psychological or psychiatric assistance, or simply does not correct his disposition, then the innocent party has the right to seek marital separation and even to accuse the marriage of nullity, especially when being denied conjugal relations by the party affected by same-sex attraction. We must help the innocent partner to be patient until the question is resolved in accord with canonical justice. If for the sake of the children, the innocent partner chooses to remain in the marriage, then he or she must be provided all possible spiritual support so that the children mature in a sound manner.

The SMCC and the Indian community give top priority to the dignity and stability of conjugal love and to the sanctity of marriage and the family bond. Indian culture upholds these as social and spiritual values. In the Indian and Christian traditions, the family is considered not so much as a private affair of the individuals involved, but as a unit within an interconnected whole. Every child is born and brought up in a wider environment of relationships, surpassing the narrow confines of the "nuclear family". Hence, though the decisive and final word is that of the individuals themselves in the selection of suitable partners, except in a few cases, marriages are generally arranged. "Arranged marriage" is a term that is quite often misunderstood by a good number of people in the West. It is not about pressure or compulsion on the part of the parents or others in the family; rather, it is a matter of the whole-hearted goodwill and gracious participation of the entire family in an important moment in the life of the son or daughter of the family. The candidates honor and trust the wisdom of the "aged" and the experienced in a stable Christian family life. This is so also because in Indian society, "marriage and family" is a serious affair that affects the peace and well-being not only of the partners concerned but also of the society at large. Many candidates themselves and parents also seek the advice of their pastors and teachers.

In those rare cases in which the individuals involved search for their own partners, they proceed with marriage only in consultation with, and with the consent and full cooperation of, the parents and their near and dear ones. The candidates themselves deem sexual purity to be a very precious gift of their own to present to their partner. However, the "priority of stability" in no way deters the Church from declaring the nullity of a marriage that is not true. Nor does the SMCC stand in the way of her sons and daughters in their choice of partners.

In the SMCC, catechizing children and young people on marriage and family takes place in regular catechetical formation programs and, intensively, in marriage preparation, where different aspects of marriage and family are dealt with at sufficient length. However, our most eminent way of catechizing all sections of our faithful on marriage and family is the very solemn sacramental celebration of the marriage itself. Besides being a celebration of the marriage of Christ and his Bride, the Church, it is also a celebration of the spiritual richness of marriage and family life grounded on lasting divine values. Family life begins at the sacramental joining together of a son and a daughter of the Church who are also "two pure souls of Christ the Bridegroom". The SMCC and her pastors are never tired of instructing the whole community of the faithful about the relation between their marriage and that of Jesus Christ with his Bride, the Church.

Let me clarify with a few anecdotes how our sacramental celebration works as the eminent catechesis on marriage and family. The couples receive the sacrament of matrimony as a saving gift of God through Christ in the sacramental (liturgical) service of the Church administered by her priest. (By the way, according to our sacramental theology of marriage, as in the case of all other sacraments, the human couple is the recipient, not the minister, of the sacrament of matrimony—which is considered a mystery.) Receiving the sacrament of matrimony, the couple is blessed, strengthened, and confirmed in living the ever life-giving mutual love and self-gift of Christ and his Bride, the Church. Let me quote three instances from the sacramental celebration of matrimony according to the Syro-Malankara Rite:

(1) The wedding ring: It is "the ring of the marriage *covenant*", and it signifies "the victorious Body and Blood, the ring that Christ, the Groom of the Church, gave his Bride". (2) In the sacramental celebration the newlyweds are crowned. This crowning reminds them of the crowning

of Christ on the Cross, where he purified and married his Bride. In their marriage, the bride and groom, who in their baptism were betrothed by Christ, are married by the crucified Christ. They are the appointed king and queen of a family of Christ the King. Their crown signifies various truths, including their victory over the evils that may threaten their married life. (3) The ultimate aim of marriage and family: the couple is led by the Church into the wedding chamber and the marriage feast so that they may uninterruptedly rejoice in the temporary chamber and the feast here on earth and be led to the heavenly chamber wherein the angels uninterruptedly taste the heavenly feast.

Briefly said, the newly married couple is prompted to live a fruitful mystical union (love at its peak and fathomless depth) in their family life, within and after the manner of the union between Christ and his Bride, the Church. They are strengthened to accept the saving truth that they take pains to protect the safety of their union by means of their joint clinging to the crucified Christ. Thus the SMCC enables the newlyweds to take their first steps and the steps that follow with this positive power. The sons and daughters of the Church seek for marriage and family life, not so that they may separate at the earliest inconvenience, but so that they may live together until death separates them.

Marriage of a son and a daughter of the SMCC is really a great event in the life of the Church. It is an event of great joy for her, because it is a celebration of the marriage of Christ and the Church and of the institution of a new "domestic church". Hence, to the extent possible, bishops are invited to officiate at the marriages in our Church. Our people appreciate the participation of many priests in the sacramental celebration of a marriage. In the first month of 2015, ten priests participated in a marriage at which I officiated. There was a young European, a friend of the bride's family. He asked some of the priests: "Why do so many priests and the Major-Archbishop-Catholicos himself participate in the wedding? Where we are from, it is uncommon to have many priests bless a marriage!" One of our priests gave him this answer: "In our Church, marriage is a great, joyful event for all concerned, including the Church, and a very decisive event for the couple and their families. We share our joy with them." The questioner responded with wonder: "Really great!" Our priests follow a similar approach in moments of sorrow and difficulties experienced by families. Participation of bishops and many priests in a burial service is not a matter of wonder! The presence of the parish priest at almost every event of small or great significance in the families who are members of his parish, his easy availability to his parishioners at any time, the personal contact with their bishops and with a large number of the faithful of their dioceses and even of other dioceses as well as the occasional visits of bishops to the parishes and families and even to the workplaces of the faithful of their dioceses really serve to attest to the place of family in the Church and to strengthen the family life of the faithful.

Yes, we realize that the marriage and family of the members of the SMCC are not totally free from the dangers of the present trends affecting the "nuclear family". We are happy that the families involved in these situations, together with the entire SMCC, try to adopt suitable "Malankarite" means to overcome the dangers, while the entire Church gladly encourages everyone to promote stronger families. In the Major Archdiocese of Trivandrum, where I am the local Ordinary, I have promised to baptize the fourth child in every family as a gesture of encouragement for the couples. I am really happy about this.

I wish to conclude this reflection by quoting a prayer of the celebrant in the sacrament of matrimony according to the Syro–Malankara Rite: "Increase their wealth of virtues; confirm them in the true faith, and assist them in handing over the faith to their children as an inheritance. By your victorious Holy Cross, O Lord, protect and watch over this bride and groom."

"Without Rupture or Discontinuity"

Paul Josef Cardinal Cordes

Pope Emeritus Benedict XVI admonished the shepherds of the Church in their teaching and pastoral ministry to maintain "communion with uninterrupted ecclesial Tradition, without breaks or temptations of irregularity".

(March 16, 2009)

It is noticeable everywhere that the upcoming session of the synod on the family is a major concern and preoccupation for ordained pastors, teachers of theology, and much of the media, too. In particular, the question about allowing the divorced and remarried to receive the sacraments is being considered and explored. So far this explosive topic seems to have overshadowed all other questions about marriage and family. Moreover, published studies and suggested solutions to this problem have stirred interest to such an astonishing degree that one might think that this was the first time anyone had ever addressed the question about allowing the divorced and remarried to receive the Eucharist. Yet this impression is not correct. The community of believers has always suffered the pains of failed marriages and for centuries has looked for justifiable ways of admitting them to the reception of Holy Communion.

A THORN IN THE FLESH OF CATHOLIC PASTORAL MINISTRY

Therefore, in preparation for the next session of the synod, we probably need to refresh our memories. History is hailed as the teacher for all branches of knowledge. What insights into theology and pastoral

Paul Josef Cardinal Cordes is president emeritus of the Pontifical Council *Cor Unum*.

practice does it have in store for the Church? The head of the household is well advised not to despise what is "old" (cf. Mt 13:52).

1. Failed Attempts to Solve the Problem

Our review can, understandably, point out only a few highlights. However, they focus, not on unimportant, peripheral events in the Church, but on essential ones, and therefore they are suggestive and significant. Although they may contribute little to a solution of the problem, they are indispensable, because they alert us to the need for caution.

Synod of the Dioceses in the German Federal Republic (1972–1975)

The plenary sessions of the Synod of Würzburg, which were drawn out over several years, dealt insistently with the "integration of remarried divorced persons in the congregations". It urged the admission of these Catholics to the reception of the sacraments under certain conditions. After a long struggle, the synod members asked the German Bishops' Conference to send a recommendation to this effect to the Apostolic See. As the synod put it, they were looking for a "loophole of mercy". A task force of bishops from the German Federal Republic, Switzerland, and Austria was then supposed to prepare a document. Professors on theological faculties who were experts on the subject were invited to join.[1] I myself was secretary of the task force, which met several times at various places. Despite all its theological and canonical acrobatics, however, the group failed to formulate a defensible recommendation. Moreover, it dawned on us that a major pastoral danger lurked in the various drafts: What effect would possible suggested solutions have on marriages in crisis? Might a concession allowing divorced and remarried persons to receive the sacraments send the wrong signal to spouses who were experiencing tensions and weaken their resolution to be faithful?

Vatican II (1962–1965)

During Vatican II, also, there was no lack of statements bringing the pain of the divorced and remarried to the attention of the Council Fathers.

---

[1] Cf. Gemeinsame Synode der Bistümer in der Bundesrepublik Deutschland, *Christlich gelebte Ehe und Familie: Einleitung* (Freiburg et al., 1976), 411–22, at 421f.

Thus, for example, on September 29, 1965 (during the Fifth Session), Archbishop Elias Zoghby, patriarchal vicar of Melkite Patriarch Maximos IV, gave a speech that attracted much notice. In it he depicted the unhappiness of broken marriages and recommended the dissolution of the marital bond in cases of adultery and malicious abandonment.

> We know how forcefully the Fathers of the Church in the Eastern Churches advised widows and widowers against entering a second marriage and thus followed the apostle's instruction. But they never withheld the right to remarry from those brides who had been wrongfully abandoned. This tradition was kept in the East, and, during the centuries of the unified Church, it was never condemned. It could be approved once again and be accepted by Catholics. A more accurate knowledge of patristics has in fact proven the existence of this teaching of the Fathers of the Eastern Church, who were no less exegetes and moral theologians than those of the West.

This opinion is unambiguous. It should also be noted, however, that one month later Maximos IV distanced himself from his vicar, saying that the latter, like all the Council Fathers, spoke merely for himself and had complete freedom to say what he thought. Then he added: "With regard to the heart of the problem, the Church must hold fast to the indissolubility of marriage."

Council of Trent (1545–1563)

The Council of Trent, too, dealt thoroughly with the problem of marriage in its deliberations. Historical investigations have demonstrated that its intention, in making the indissolubility of the marital bond a dogma, was to defend the Church's authority and, consequently, the binding character of her doctrine. Of course, these statements are not immediately concerned with the admission of the divorced and remarried to the sacraments. Within the context of our question, they do not give even the slightest hint that the pastors of the Church could on their own authority disregard God's word in problematic cases.[2]

---

[2] Waldemar Molinski, *Theologie der Ehe in der Geschichte* (Aschaffenburg: Pattloch, 1976), 152–58. An especially thorough and reliable study of the Council's formulation and intention can be found in Andreas Wollbold, *Pastoral mit wiederverheirateten Geschiedenen: gordischer Knoten oder ungeahnte Möglichkeiten?* (Regensburg: Verlag Friedrich Pustet, 2015), 107–18.

Medieval penitential manuals

In the middle of the first millennium, a great number of instructions for the sacrament of reconciliation were written down. They originated in Irish, Anglo-Saxon, and Scottish monasteries, and missionary monks brought them to the European mainland together with the practice of auricular confession. From the fifth century on, they served to varying degrees as a central pastoral guideline and were influential at least until the *Decretum Gratiani* (1140).[3] They also note our problem. But in them the reader seeks in vain a generally acknowledged solution to it.

Patristic writings

Finally, it is almost impossible to count the authors and instructions bequeathed to the Church in patristic writings on the subject of marital teaching.[4] To name just a few: the *Shepherd of Hermas* (written around 155), Clement of Alexandria (d. 215), Hilary of Poitiers (d. 366), Basil the Great (d. 379), Jerome (d. 389), Augustine (d. 430), Pope Innocent I (d. 417), and Pope Gregory the Great (d. 604). In all these writings, we can discern a warning against laxism as the basic theme. The indissolubility of marriage is inculcated; often there is a clear doctrinal defense against any "more lenient practice". In the Western Church, no practicable way of approving a possible remarriage is found. This finding is proved not only by individual citations from the above-mentioned authors but also by specialized systematic studies.[5]

Summary

This review of Church history gives little reason to hope that the most recent attempts and opinions have now found the "philosopher's stone". Even though their proponents are brimming with self-confidence, like men on a mission, and can be assured of the applause

---

[3] Peter Manns dedicated a thorough study to them; see Norbert Wetzel, *Die öffentlichen Sünder oder Soll die Kirche Ehen scheiden?* (Mainz: Matthias Grünewald Verlag, 1970), 42–75 and 275–302.

[4] Marie-Joseph Rouët de Journel, S.J., ed., *Enchiridion patristicum* (Barcelona: Herder, 1956).

[5] For example, Gilles Pelland, S.J., "La pratica della Cheisa antica relativa ai fedeli divorziati risposati", in Congregazione per la Dottrina della Fede, ed., *Documenti, commenti e studi* 17 (Vatican City: Libreria Editrice Vaticana, 1998), 99–131.

of the media, any careful and thoughtful observer will be skeptical about their suggestions.

2. Misguided Models

These findings from Church history no doubt diminish our confidence that we can find a way out of the dilemma between required doctrine and pastoral sensitivity. On the other hand, some current suggestions that claim to solve the problem are extremely odd. One wonders why the authors who propose them would risk the academic reputation of an entire discipline.

"Paradigm shift"

After the conclusion of the spring plenary session of the German Bishops' Conference (February 24, 2015), the head of the Pastoral Commission of this conference, Bishop Franz-Josef Hermann Bode, spoke to the press. He is one of the elected delegates for the next session of the synod of bishops. His intention was to scrutinize the moral theological and pastoral dimension of the problem and to elevate it to the level of systematic theology. Pastoral practice and dogma, said the bishop, who holds a degree in dogmatic theology, have to be mutually enriching in this case. He boils down this speculation to a "historically important" insight, which he even calls a "paradigm shift". Then he brings in the heavy artillery and cites the conciliar constitution *Gaudium et spes*. In the very first paragraph we read that "Nothing genuinely human fails to raise an echo in their hearts" (that is, in the hearts of Christ's disciples). From this the bishop now concludes: "Not only must the Christian message resonate among people, but people must resonate among us." Later he explains his new perspective again in an interview. In it he calls it a fundamental theological question: "What relationship does the doctrine of the Church still have today to people's everyday lives? In our doctrine do we take sufficiently into account the concrete experiences of people? Doctrine and life must not be completely separate from one another." Thus, under the heading of "paradigm shift", he heralds the revival of the old claim that orthodoxy is dependent on orthopraxis.

Indeed, the attempt to derive dogmatic content from human experience is not all that new. While the Vatican II Constitution on the

Church in the Modern World was being drafted, the Council Fathers considered it and thoroughly settled the question.[6] At that time, the question revolved around the relevance to the faith of societal or ecclesiastical phenomena, and it seized upon the biblical expression "signs of the times": "Do we see or hear God's instruction or voice in these signs? Can we interpret them as theological truth?" This question became an important starting point for the *aggiornamento* to which the Council was devoted, as everyone knows. The result of the deliberations was that it would be a mistake to *search out* these "signs of the times" in people's lives as a "source of the faith"—as no. 11 had originally been formulated. Rather, such signs should be *discerned* (*discernere*). In this way the Council Fathers explained that brand new events and needs of Christians served as an impetus for the pastors of the Church to set them in the light of faith, to test them, and to give an answer on the basis of revealed truth. They expressly ruled out the distressing, overhasty conclusion that a phenomenon that challenged the Church was per se already a source of faith (*locus theologicus*).

Moreover, the conciliar Constitution on Divine Revelation (*Dei Verbum*) itself leaves no doubt about the fact that the faith of the Catholic Church comes solely from Sacred Scripture and the Church's doctrine (*DV 5*). Finally, it would be quite paradoxical to set aside these unequivocal instructions and to try to assign to a small group of Church members, who are living in a spiritually lamentable yet objectively irregular situation, the role of being a source of faith. Bishop Bode's call for a change of perspective is therefore neither original nor helpful.

Ludicrous theories

Finally, we must mention two opinions that apply such astonishing theological "reasoning" that one can only rub one's eyes in amazement. With regard to the remarriage of baptized persons, a professor on the Catholic faculty of a German university writes: "I start instead from a generative concept of sacrament that dissolves the boundaries of the sacrament of matrimony. The first sacramental marriage continues to

---

[6]Joseph Ratzinger reports at length on how the Council Fathers dealt with this question; see commentary on no. 11 of this constitution in: *Lexikon für Theologie und Kirche*, supplementary vol. 3 (Freiburg: Herder, 1968), 313–54.

exist, but the actual rupture does not destroy the indestructible character of God's promise of fidelity but, rather, activates God's promise once again" (Otmar Fuchs). Through this speculation, the "second marriage" is interpreted as a specific source of grace!

Another author interprets 1 Corinthians 11:29ff., in which the apostle demands that the faithful examine themselves: "For any one who eats and drinks [of the Lord's Body and Blood] without discerning the body eats and drinks judgment upon himself. That is why many of you are weak and ill, and some have died." Willibald Sandler does not take this demand by Paul as a warning against the unworthy reception of the Eucharist; instead, he assumes that the apostle is recommending unworthy reception because it "tends not toward damnation but toward salvation".[7]

THE FOUNDATION OF MARRIAGE: GOD'S WORD

The confusion of contemporary voices that are trying to contribute toward a solution to the problem makes it necessary to take another look at the binding source of our faith. Therefore, we must mention, if only briefly, the instructions given by divine revelation concerning the indissolubility of marriage.

Sacred Scripture and the early Church

In the three synoptic Gospels (Mk 10:11–12; Mt 5:31f. and 19:9; Lk 16:18), the Lord recalls God's original, unalloyed will and very clearly commands the exclusivity and permanence of every marital bond. Although these words are addressed primarily to Christians with Jewish roots, the Apostle to the Gentiles teaches them to the formerly pagan Christian communities in the First Letter to the Corinthians (7:10). He expressly cites as his authority the aforementioned command of the Lord; nowhere can the possibility of a second marriage be found. Biased exegetes maintain that we can conclude from this passage in the letter that Paul also allows for divorce; after all, he writes, this time citing his own authority: "But if the unbelieving partner desires to separate, let

---

[7]Both citations are found in Georg Augustin and Ingo Proft, eds., *Ehe und Familie: Wege zum Gelingen aus katholischer Perspektive* (Freiburg: Herder, 2014), 391 and 418, respectively.

it be so; in such a case the brother or sister is not bound [like a slave]" (7:15). But this interpretation works only because it ignores the fact that the dissolution of the marital bond that Paul permits here is intended to safeguard the faith of Christians; by no means does it intend to concede possible compromises in cases of common difficulties between spouses. In this respect, the so-called Pauline Privilege is actually an intensification of the Lord's teaching: A Christian should not turn his marital bond into a formality or uphold it at the expense of his faith; indeed, the faith takes priority—the faith that, according to Christ's word, includes the indissolubility of marriage.

Anyone who derives the "loophole of mercy" from Paul's command must ultimately ask himself the question: Where does he get the right to supplement Jesus' command with the apostle's authority?

Usually interpreters grant to this saying of Jesus the force of a challenge and no more. Yet it cannot be reduced to a friendly admonition. Otherwise, we misconstrue the understanding of the early Church. The young Christian community regarded the verses in question as law-making. It grasped the fact: Someone who breaks marital unity and enters a new union is not acting according to God's will; he commits adultery. Already in the Old Testament, Yahweh had spoken through the prophet Malachi against divorce: "For I hate divorce, says the LORD the God of Israel, and covering one's garment with violence, says the LORD of hosts. So take heed to yourselves and do not be faithless" (2:16).

In apostolic times, the explicit prohibition of remarriage applied at first to the husband with respect to all women. From the fourth century on, then, there was a tendency to put husband and wife on equal footing canonically: Matthew 5:32 no longer applied to the husband alone. In the wake of this equal treatment of men and women, if we then apply the same prohibition of divorce to the wife, we can conclude from it: No one—neither man nor woman—may marry someone who is divorced. That comes very close in practice, if not terminologically as well, to separation from bed, board, and cohabitation. Therefore, no canonical solution is so close to the teaching in Matthew as the Catholic solution. The Protestant exegete Ulrich Lutz writes:

> The Catholic position, which foresees the possibility of separation from bed, board, and cohabition with a continuing *vinculum* of marriage, in my opinion, comes especially close to the position expressed in Matthew....

The decisive point at which Matthew and Catholic practice converge is in the prohibition against marrying a divorced woman. This corresponds to the denial of a second marriage, which the Fathers of the Church as a whole upheld very decisively; not until the fourth century did a change begin in the East.[8]

Unequivocal, binding teaching

Divine revelation, therefore, is opposed to the "more lenient practice" so often sought; references to God's mercy, to epikeia, or to a division between canon law and pastoral practice are limited by the words of Jesus. Indeed, ecclesiastical order remains dependent on the Gospel and must not twist it. Those who have divorced and then remarried have transgressed Jesus' unequivocal command; they are living in a situation that objectively contradicts God's will and, therefore, cannot go to Holy Communion. An identical instruction was given by the Vatican Congregation for the Doctrine of the Faith just recently in a letter dated September 14, 1994, which, because of the continuity and the reliability of Church doctrine, must not be disregarded even in the synod.[9]

An "audit" of Church history on this subject proves to be decidedly unencouraging. Although sought down through the centuries, no promising point of departure appears for a "solution" that took revelation seriously and had no dangerous effects on existing marriages. Anyone who goes around the parishes saying that the long-sought-after "loophole of mercy" has been found has shut his eyes to the aforementioned dead ends in Church history. Or else he is pretentiously self-confident: as though today suddenly such an ingenious theological insight had been discovered that it would open up a path that had been blocked for two thousand years.

Divorced and remarried persons have been and are today a cause of anguish for the Church and her pastoral ministry. Nevertheless, it is obviously not in her power to heal it. And anyone who tries nevertheless

---

[8] So he writes in his commentary *Das Evangelium nach Matthäus (Mt 1–7)*, Evangelisch-Katholischer Kommentar zum Neuen Testament, vol. 1/1 (Düsseldorf: Benziger/Neukirchener, 2002), 365–66.

[9] See Congregation for the Doctrine of the Faith, *Letter to the Bishops of the Catholic Church concerning the Reception of Holy Communion by the Divorced and Remarried Members of the Faithful*, September 14, 1994. The text of the letter can be found in English and Latin in Robert Dodaro, O.S.A., ed., *Remaining in the Truth of Christ: Marriage and Communion in the Catholic Church* (San Francisco: Ignatius Press, 2014), 264–79.

to formulate guidelines for admitting such persons to the sacraments soon runs into the question of whether "general norms" are at all conceivable in this area. As the commission appointed by the "Synod of German Dioceses" proved, not only would that be a Sisyphean task; there is no guarantee that such rules would not be abused. The "extreme case" would easily become the norm, and there would be nothing left of "the essence of the Christians and Church".[10]

A CONSTRUCTIVE DIGRESSION

Plainly the problem of the divorced and remarried receiving the sacraments requires sympathetic pastors to find a solution. And this reassurance is not offered here as a self-serving declaration; no one should be discredited if he tries to find a remedy. Nevertheless, so much has been made recently of the plight of those concerned that public opinion in the Church seems to be traumatized by it, or at least fixated on it. The courage to cut the Gordian knot is declared to be the most important order of the present hour, bar none.

Cooler heads try to get some perspective. Ordained pastors are commanded to proclaim to their dioceses and congregations all adversities, pitfalls, and opportunities—even things that are perhaps forgotten on account of sympathy with the afflicted. Because the spirit of the world always obscures or disputes matters of faith.

Then, too, often the matter serves to bring about a rediscovery and changes the perspective. Even old things may appear in a new light. The apostle expects the Thessalonians to "test everything; hold fast what is good" (1 Thess 5:21). In the struggle to allow the divorced and remarried to receive the Eucharist, constructive aspects turn up that can be integrated into the existing Church order. They must not be overlooked in our zeal. We will mention two, which are possible even without theological somersaults.

1. The Promise of Fidelity

A few weeks ago I was asked to approach the spiritual burden of divorced persons from an angle that until now has not been mentioned often. A

---

[10]Hans Urs von Balthasar, "Temporary Christians", in Balthasar, *Elucidations*, trans. John Riches (San Francisco: Ignatius Press, 1998), 298–308, at 302.

German lawyer, Rainer Beckmann, had written down a detailed testimony that makes clear an oft-forgotten aspect of the problem of divorce. He intended to publish a book of his reflections stating the reasons why, after the failure of his marriage, he had not entered a new union. He had decided to remain faithful to the promise that he had made at his wedding. He asked me to write a foreword.

An exceptional case?

The manuscript that he sent to me is now in print.[11] In many passages the author takes to task the two reports with which Walter Cardinal Kasper started off the discussion at the Consistory in February 2014. He also analyzes critically many answers of the German Bishops' Conference to the questionnaire of the Roman Secretariat of the Synod of Bishops. The author sagaciously sheds light on current theses and views and rejects many of them, yet even more impressively he wins over the reader by his honesty. It is moving to witness how he struggles in faith to arrive at the decision to be faithful to the promise that he made when he received the sacrament of matrimony. He is able, discreetly, to involve the reader in his way of the cross. The following excerpts from the beginning of his account are no substitute for a personal reading of his testimony.

After almost twenty-five years of married life together, Rainer Beckmann's wife began a relationship with another man in early 2010. In the summer of 2010, she moved out; in 2012, she got a divorce and married her new partner in a civil ceremony in late 2013. The abandoned husband experienced these events as a family tragedy. "For me the break-up of our family was the biggest catastrophe of my life.... My wife and I for many years had led a married life that in our social circle was perceived as altogether 'exemplary' and decidedly Christian." Both spouses participated actively in parish life, and they took the Christian education of their four children to heart.

While his wife rushed into a new relationship, the author of the book saw no way to continue his own sex life. It was quite clear to him that at his Catholic wedding he had bound himself indissolubly to his wife. He had never seriously considered that this marriage might also fail. "So there was no Plan B." Instead, he wrestled with the question of whether and

---

[11] Rainer Beckmann, *Das Evangelium der ehelichen Treue: Eine Antwort auf Kardinal Kasper* (Kisslegg: Fe-medienverlag, 2015).

how long he should fight for a reconciliation with his wife. At the same time, he began to hear from other people arguments that were supposed to console and encourage him. Even Catholic acquaintances advised him to forget the past and to accept the divorce. Why was he not thinking of a new relationship? In it he could no doubt find "new happiness".

For a while he wrestled with his faith. And it took him several weeks before he was able to arrive at a clear decision. "A 'second marriage' was not 'only' contrary to Christ's command and Church teaching, but also and above all against *my own marriage vow*. It was clear and unambiguous. I had promised my wife solemnly and in the presence of God that I would love and honor her 'until death do us part'. If that was meant seriously on my wedding day, then I was obliged and willing to abide by it."

Then the author of this testimony again addresses his readers directly. Many people would not be able to agree with his way of seeing things because they lack the religious basis for doing so. After all, people's decisions are guided by the standards of secular society, for which marriage is a civil-law contract subject to termination. The Catholic Church, however, has another understanding of it. It "regards the lifelong union of husband and wife as a sacrament that reflects God's fidelity and his love for his people and the loving devotion of Christ to his Church. I am convinced that this interpretation is correct, and at my wedding I also gave my consent along these lines."

The author does not publish his confession light-heartedly. He is aware that the marital bond concerns only three persons: himself, his wife, and God. Furthermore, he shows his esteem for his wife by expressing his apprehension that he might offend her by going public. Nevertheless, he decides to publish his account. For he takes the position—and he is certainly right—that without his testimony an important voice would be missing in the debate about divorced and remarried persons. He is trying to bring the oft-forgotten "third person" into the picture. God is also the reason why he reached the painful decision not to start a new relationship with a woman. To put it briefly and simply, we could say that his faith bound him to fidelity, to stake his life on God, and to accept the truth of God's word without compromise.

Lessons learned

This is why throughout his book he also refrains from tracing his family problem back to secondary causes—for instance, to "the Church's inability to speak", to a sex-saturated society, or to old-fashioned Catholic moral teaching. Rather, it is the "lack of a sense of faith" ("the problem behind the problem") that he emphatically challenges ordained pastors to confront. This problem, however, cannot be resolved by "relaxing" discipline.

A less strict discipline would, instead, lead to a further watering down of the relationship to God. The book then lists the ways in which this would trivialize the faith: farewell to marital fidelity, doubts about the correctness of Church teaching about marriage, reception of the Eucharist without proper dispositions, the devaluation of the sacrament of penance, the promotion of religious relativism, and the distortion of the concept of "mercy". Nevertheless, the author does not condemn those who have not maintained the fidelity they promised, and he also mentions options that pastoral care makes available to the divorced and remarried.

Relevance

The author of this publication deserves first of all special attention, because, amid the flurry of commentaries on the synod by bishops and the media, he states an important truth: remarriage is not a "must" for divorced persons. This point is not infrequently drowned out in the heated debate. And it is perhaps even unpopular among those who consider themselves the really merciful ones (and paradoxically emphasize "mercy" to the exclusion of all else). So this voice reminds the Church and all of us about an important truth. The importance of his contribution is confirmed and reinforced from a completely unexpected quarter.

The sociology of knowledge has thoroughly investigated the development and persistence of intellectual notions and behavioral impulses among human beings. It is a secular science, and we must not accuse it of having a distorting bias. Consequently, its insights can no doubt make a claim to validity in the pastoral marriage debate, too.

Researchers have discovered that our convictions and ways of acting are generally copied from others. *Through social interaction*, they become rooted in our awareness, or "internalized", as they say. In this process, we make not only the arguments but also the life-styles of our fellow-men our own. It is plain, however, that in adopting these things, not all models have the same influence on us; this depends rather on the human and intellectual caliber of the others. Of course, if we encounter authentic persons, they communicate to us an emphatic, deeply felt certainty about our judgments and actions.

It would be fatal for all of us if neither messages nor testimonies made it clear that fidelity to the promise once made is possible even after the failure of a marriage. It would be fatal for all of us if ordained pastors busied themselves only with the so-called new solutions and there were no divorced persons who kept the promise of fidelity they had once made. The sociology of knowledge leaves no doubt about it: Whatever no longer appears in word and deed first becomes irrelevant and then is forgotten.[12]

There is yet another reason to give a special hearing in the ongoing discussion to the voice cited here: someone who has clearly complied with God's will acquires greater spiritual authority in the Church. He has on his side more than the psychological power of his existential testimony. Speaking in his favor also—although to a lesser degree—is what the Church believes about the great figures in her history: that they are closer to God's designs for this Church. They follow the eternal Shepherd; "they know his voice" (Jn 10:4), and they can make it out, despite the high noise level.

The author sums up:

> Therefore it is important to witness credibly to the indissolubility of marriage in the future, too: as Church in teaching, as a Catholic Christian in one's personal life. A spouse who despite divorce complies with the indissolubility of marriage gives witness to his personal faith and to the faith of the whole Church. Even more important is the witness of those who live their married life together in faith and thus set before our eyes a real likeness of Christ's fidelity to his Church. Only on this basis is it possible to witness credibly to "the vocation and mission of the family in the Church and contemporary world"—which is the motto of the upcoming session of the synod.

2. Spiritual Communion

Even though the upcoming assembly of the world's bishops in Rome is supposed to deal with the full spectrum of family issues, it was at first primarily occupied with the reception of the Eucharist by divorced

---

[12] Cf. Peter L. Berger and Thomas Luckmann, *The Social Construction of Reality: A Treatise in the Sociology of Knowledge* (London: Penguin Books, 1966), 65ff.

and remarried persons. One reason for this is that the drift of Cardinal Kasper's introductory reports captured everyone's attention with this problem. For various motives it was so decisively brought to the fore that without further inquiry as to the number of those affected and its relevance for all the local Churches in the Universal Church, it likewise appeared to be the most urgent problem.

Furthermore—and problematically—no room was allowed for consideration of another personal encounter with the Lord, for instance, "spiritual communion". When I brought this up after the introductory report, it was in the speaker's view not even an aspect of the difficulty that needs to be resolved. His comment on the idea of recommending spiritual communion to the divorced and remarried was short and simple: Someone who should not be admitted to the sacramental-symbolic reception of the Eucharist would not be worthy of spiritual communion, either.

Did the speaker oppose a merely spiritual encounter with the Lord so categorically because it would weaken his main argument, that divine mercy must decide on admission to the Lord's table? Was the circumvention of an alternative merely supposed to prevent the spearhead in the battle for the consumption of the Eucharistic food from becoming blunt? Or was ignorance about the act of spiritual communion ultimately a factor? The fact is, after all, that even the 1992 *Catechism of the Catholic Church* no longer contains the expression, and this ecclesial textbook certainly does not explain this form of communion or recommend it to the faithful.

Johannes Auer, former professor of dogmatic theology in Regensburg, was probably one of the last writers who demonstrated its theological roots and the benefits thereof in deepening one's personal relationship with Christ.[13]

The sacrament

The theologian starts with the premise that the celebration of the Lord's Supper with its fruit, the Holy Eucharist, is the greatest sacrament of the

---

[13]Johannes Auer, "Geistige Kommunion: Sinn und Praxis der communio spiritualis und ihre Bedeutung für unsere Zeit", in *Geist und Leben* 24 (1951): 113–32; available online, along with the citations. I have also discussed the topic of "spiritual communion" in a booklet entitled *Geistige Kommunion—befreit vom Staub der Jahrhunderte*, 2nd ed. (Kisslegg: Fe-Medienverlags, 2015).

New Covenant. In various passages, the New Testament gives reasons for the dignity and the value of the bread that is transformed into the Body of Christ and given to us as food. It is not necessary to prove this fact here. The reception of Holy Communion is a means of obtaining and securing our eternal life; furthermore, it involves the faithful in Christ's own sacrifice and makes the baptized one Body in the Risen Lord.

Over the centuries, besides these theological statements of fact, the idea becomes increasingly prominent that the Eucharist is a physical encounter with the Person of Jesus. This view of the sacramental event emphasizes its grace-filled and mystical side.

The Greek theologians Basil (d. 379) and Gregory Nazianzen (d. 390) see blessing with the Spirit of God as a further effect of receiving Communion; Hilary of Poitiers (d. 367) describes partaking of Christ in the Eucharist as a communication in the life of the Trinity. John Chrysostom (d. 407) scrutinizes the empirical dimension of receiving Communion. He concludes from Paul's saying about "discerning the body" (1 Cor 11:29) that the sacramental effect is not necessarily identical to the physical action; the food must be received in faith by a believer. This brings to light the fact that the symbolic eating of the Body of Christ is not self-contained; it is directed instead toward interior graces and spiritual fruits.

Spiritual encounter with the Lord

This leads to a second theological line of inquiry in early Christianity; the spiritual effect of the physical partaking becomes prominent. Tertullian (d. after 220) and Cyprian (d. 258) already pointed out the limits of the merely sacramental-symbolic eating of the Lord's Body and emphasized the spiritual effect of Communion. The Greek theologians Basil and Gregory Nazianzen teach, furthermore, that the Eucharist imparts the Spirit of Christ. Other Church Fathers, such as Ambrose (d. 397), Gregory of Nyssa (d. 394), or John Chrysostom (d. 407), stress that in this sacrament there is a reality that cannot be grasped at all by the senses; this sacrament must be received in faith, that is, by those who are spirit-filled. The great Augustine (d. 430) is especially significant. On one occasion, in speaking to the newly baptized, he emphasizes in his marvelous formula for administering the Holy Eucharist the empirical, palpable dependence of the Lord's Supper on community: "When you hear 'the Body of Christ', you reply 'Amen'. Be a member of Christ's Body, then, so that your Amen may ring true!... Be what you see; receive what you are."[14] But he is also the one who relativizes the sacramental-symbolic meal and underscores the spiritual encounter with the Lord. In his poignant language he takes this truth to extremes. His sermons on the Gospel of John contain the sentence that is most often quoted with regard to our topic: "Ut quid paras dentes et ventrem? Crede, et manducasti!"[15] "Why are you getting your teeth and stomach ready? Believe, and you have eaten!" Such an appeal to spiritualize the reception of the Eucharist is unsurpassable and becomes a pivotal point for the idea of "spiritual communion" over its long and far-reaching history.

Until Emperor Constantine's edict of tolerance (312), the faithful had celebrated Holy Mass in the close circle of those who after a long catechumenate and often in times of persecution of Christians had reached spiritual maturity. Now though, on account of the new freedom and State recognition, many people whose personal decision for the faith was less radical were streaming into the congregations. People began participating in the celebration of the Eucharist without eating the Lord's Body, too. As a result of the migration of peoples and the mission to the Germanic tribes, there was a diminished understanding of the language of the liturgy; the congregation was less able to follow the prayers and actions of the priest and increasingly interpreted the ceremony allegorically and symbolically. For all these reasons, the number of those who encountered the Lord *realiter* in the sacrament diminished; people were content to draw close to him in a spiritual way.

In the Middle Ages, the Eucharistic Jesus was often seen as the guest of the soul, as the King whom one goes out to greet, whom one addresses in personal conversation as an intimate friend. Bernard of Clairvaux (d. 1153), with the bridal mysticism of the Canticle of Canticles, Bonaventure (d. 1274), and the mystics of the fourteenth century, such as the German Heinrich Seuse (d. 1366), contributed much to the spread of individualized reception of the Eucharist. The Renaissance brought with it an increasingly anthropocentric and egocentric world view that led more and more to the atrophy of the communal and eschatological meaning of the Eucharistic action.

This one-sided emphasis on the interior and intimate aspects of Holy Communion no longer did justice to the theological richness of the Eucharistic action. The thought of being incorporated into Christ's great

---

[14] Saint Augustine, Sermon 272.
[15] Saint Augustine, *Commentary on the Gospel of John* 25,12.

redemptive sacrifice was entirely lost. The liturgy forfeited its celebratory character and its overall joy about Christ's victory and Resurrection. What remained was a "spiritual communion" in which the individual aspect of the Christ encounter was bundled together, so to speak. Yet it caused the fullness of the liturgy, the symbolic character of the sacrament, and its reference to the community to atrophy.

Less frequent reception of Holy Communion

Moreover, a greater sensitivity to sin had the effect of making the reception of the Eucharist under the species of bread less frequent. Wars, plague, and other epidemics afflicted the people and often appeared to them as God's punishment for their transgressions. They took to heart the words of the Apostle to the Gentiles to the Church in Corinth, that God would not allow unworthy participation in the Eucharistic meal to go unpunished. He told them that weakness, sickness, and death were the consequences of the unworthy reception of the Eucharist: "For any one who eats and drinks without discerning the body eats and drinks judgment upon himself. That is why many of you are weak and ill, and some have died" (1 Cor 11:29f). For "spiritual communion", however, the aspect of unworthiness did not apply. Anyone who desired it was not affected by Paul's warning.

Finally, another factor in the tendency to stay away from the Lord's table that should not be overlooked is the alienation from the faith that caused people to regard "the sacred action [of the Church] surpassing all others"[16] (as Vatican II put it) as nothing but a burdensome duty. In any case, it is typical that this led to the formulation of a precept of the Church: Catholics had to be required to receive Holy Communion at least once a year.

This very condensed history of the development of "spiritual communion" shows that the spread of it no doubt had its dark side. Yet there is no mistaking the fact that the practice is altogether legitimate theologically, and its salutary effects over the centuries are indisputable. The Decrees of the Council of Trent (1545–1563) and the *Roman Catechism* (1567), therefore, mention it and hold fast to it. It grants a share in Christ's sacrifice through faith, yearning, and love. Its spiritual fruit

[16]Second Vatican Council, Constitution on the Sacred Liturgy, *Sacrosanctum concilium* (December 4, 1963), 7.

is, in the estimation of ecclesiastical authority, almost the same as that of sacramental Communion.

Of course while arguing for the promotion of a spiritual form of encountering Christ, we must not forget that God's salvific work can be grasped in an earthly way. Both the Incarnation of the Son of God and the sacramental structure of the Church use, in behalf of God's redemptive work, elements that are perceptible to our senses: words that we can hear and signs that we can see and touch. Redemption must not be banished to a spiritual back room; it does not flee into mystical darkness. Yet to recall this palpability is by no means to equate the "exterior" and the "interior" of man indiscriminately.

Limits of the law

Herein lies also the real snag in Cardinal Kasper's verdict. He is on the wrong track when he concludes that those who are canonically prohibited from receiving Communion are unworthy of "spiritual communion" as well. For canon law, which in our case denies admission to Communion, and the religious disposition of a heart, on the other hand, are two completely different things. As is generally known, law, even in the Church, can regulate only empirically evident acts and omissions. It cannot judge the situation of a person's soul and does not claim to do so. Therefore, according to Church law, the prohibition against receiving Communion applies precisely to so-called "public" sinners. The interior longing of a believer to be united with the Lord, in contrast, is determined on the level of personal piety, and ultimately this cannot be judged reliably from outside. Many divorced and remarried persons believe that they are subjectively justified—and in God's sight they may be; others know that they are guilty and precisely for that reason want to encounter the Lord. Such an interior attitude is beyond the reach of canon law. And, accordingly, the Church's pastors are forbidden to subject the decisions made by these persons in their hearts to such conditions, which in the case of more public acts are canonically relevant. As the Pontifical Council for the Interpretation of Legislative Texts expressly states,[17]

---

[17] Pontifical Council for Legislative Texts, *Declaration II: Concerning the Admission to Holy Communion of Faithful Who Are Divorced and Remarried*, June 24, 2000. Italian text published in *L'Osservatore Romano*, July 7, 2000, p. 1, and *Communicationes* 32 (2000), 159–62. The text of the *Declaration* can be found in English and Latin in Dodaro, *Remaining in the Truth of Christ*, 281–85.

canon law in this matter judges only the external, socially observable situation of those in question, not their subjective, interior aspirations. This restriction, finally, is also covered by a basic conviction in Church law: an old canonical axiom says: "De internis non iudicat Ecclesia"; "The Church does not judge the interior disposition."

Tradition as teacher

As with the survey of earlier efforts to find pastoral responses to the plight of the divorced and remarried, a brief review of the tradition of "spiritual communion" also produces a noteworthy insight: Through many centuries of ups and downs in sacramental practice, it was a valuable approach to fellowship with the living Lord. It deserves to be rediscovered.

Certainly, the problem of Holy Communion for the divorced and remarried should not and cannot be solved by stressing it; anyway, this very complex drama cannot be ended in a quick verbal skirmish. Yet by no means can "spiritual communion" be ruled out for those members of the lay faithful who are canonically impeded from receiving the sacraments yet long for a personal encounter with Jesus Christ. In pastoral practice, too, our memory is short. As recently as 1947, the encyclical on the liturgy, *Mediator Dei* by Pope Pius XII, contains the exhortation: "[The Church] wishes in the first place that Christians—especially when they cannot easily receive holy communion—should do so at least by desire."[18]

Proclaiming the truth about "spiritual communion" is first of all a pastoral service to those who cannot participate in the liturgy itself. Certainly, if they are old or sick, knowing about it and being encouraged to receive Holy Communion "spiritually" would often be a joy and a consolation. Many of them seek Christ's face in their private prayer or by reading Sacred Scripture; many watch or listen to broadcasts of Sunday Mass as a way of begging for the power of the Lord's Resurrection. As Communion is being distributed, should they not be instructed by the off-camera commentator to receive Christ spiritually? Among Catholics in Italy, set prayers are still commonly recited that ask for this kind of much-desired encounter with the Lord. Although it seems to be forgotten worldwide, it should again have a place in the proclamation of the faith and in catechesis.

---

[18] Pope Pius XII, encyclical letter *Mediator Dei* (November 20, 1947), 117.

Our relationship with God is bound up with our interior life. Without the contribution of the heart, pious activity remains "a noisy gong or a clanging cymbal"—as the Apostle to the Gentiles says about human love. That is why since the fifth century (*Sacramentarium Leonianum*) the priest prays silently, with folded hands, at Mass after his own Communion: "Quod ore sumpsi, Domine, mente capiam": "What has passed my lips as food, O Lord, may I possess in purity of heart."

It is not enough for the believer to perform the sacramental rubrics correctly. External numerical repetition even jeopardizes the depth and seriousness of sacramental reception. The Roman proverb, *Cottidiana vilescunt*, "Doing things every day leads to superficiality", applies also to the Most Blessed Sacrament. Consequently, theological knowledge about "spiritual communion" could lend new seriousness to our approach to the table of the Lord, so that we follow the apostle Paul's instruction and "discern the body (of Christ)". Someone who has allowed himself to be formed by the teaching about "spiritual communion" is better equipped to resist the ritualism that empties the liturgy of meaning.

The trustworthy steward (1 Cor 4:2)

Those who hold office in the Church are commissioned to provide pastoral care in the parishes and dioceses. They have as the model for their mission the Lord himself, who is close to his flock, leads them carefully, knows them, calls them by name individually, and even lays down his life for them (cf. Jn 10). How could ordained pastors remain unmoved by the cares and sufferings that afflict their faithful? Only someone who knows his flock and shares its burdens follows the example of Jesus.

In this ministry, of course, they cannot just rely on their own compassion. They must not be led astray by the clash of opinions or allow their secular surroundings to dictate the terms of their faith—however insistent the media may be. Again, the Apostle to the Gentiles gives us a reliable orientation. In the above-cited First Letter to the Corinthians, he briefly discusses his understanding of himself as a "steward of the mysteries of God". He is a "servant of Christ", not his independent collaborator. Paul knows that he is radically dependent on the Lord and unconditionally subject to him. Therefore, he even rules out the possibility of being evaluated at all by human beings. The apostle gruffly and severely allows no one except the Lord to judge his trustworthy activity. He does not care about the applause meter; he is immune to such considerations—what an exemplary shepherd! "With me it is a very small thing that I should be judged by you or by any human court."[19]

May faith like this guide the spirit of the upcoming synod!

[19] 1 Cor 4:1–3. See also Wolfgang Schrage, *Der erste Brief an die Korinther (1 Kor 1,1–6,11)*, Evangelisch-Katholischer Kommentar zum Neuen Testament, vol.7/1 (Zürich: Benziger–Neukirchener, 1991), 318ff.

Reflections on the Family

Dominik Cardinal Duka, O.P.

The convocation of the synod on the family has aroused a lot of unexpected attention. It has provoked stormy debates and has revealed a certain polarity between Church and society. We may be surprised, scandalized, or even saddened by it. These are understandable attitudes toward the reality, that is, toward the long and serious crisis of the family, which, we can say with certainty, was already doomed to destruction by the end of the first half of the nineteenth century. Anyone who has read the *Communist Manifesto* will agree with me. Do we understand the significance of this ideological pressure that has lasted for more than a century and a half? Not only readers and students are exposed to this ideology, but also the hundreds of millions of the earth's inhabitants living under totalitarian dictatorships. The family has been pilloried as an exploitative institution, as a place that oppresses spontaneity and destroys hedonistic desire, individual liberty, and so on. Indeed, the Marxist concept of class struggle has become a tool of depth psychology as well, in countries where the confessor has been replaced by therapists, psychologists, or psychiatrists, and the logical consequence of this has been the rejection of the family. If we look at current popular culture, cinema, and literature, we can tell that they are working through their Oedipus and Electra complexes, creating those rich and impassioned plots which, however, influence the consumers of such cultural artifacts in ways that are sure to harm the family. I think, though, that the uproar caused by the synod may be, from a certain perspective, a positive signal as well. It tells us that the family is a challenge even today. It causes scandal and anxiety—in short, it does not allow anyone to remain indifferent, not even those who say that the family belongs to the past or is coming to an end.

Dominik Cardinal Duka, O.P., is the archbishop of Prague.

This description of the situation does not accurately express the discussion that is going on within the synods, above all with regard to the question of annulments and to Holy Communion for the divorced and remarried. My opinion is that the current crisis of the family is closely connected with the destruction of anthropology, that is, of our understanding of human beings as such. Let us pause for a few moments to examine the basic elements at work today in the common understanding of man and to consider which of these elements we should set aside.

For those who live in the religious indifference of the postmodern era, what does the concept of man mean? Is he the image of God? We know that it is not easy to speak about God if the original of the copy or image, that is, God himself, as Sacred Scripture says, is invisible, unimaginable, and unfathomable. Similarly, today we can see this problem in the rejection expressed by abstract art. If Being is for the most part invisible, if we cannot touch it, if we cannot grasp it with the senses, then in society, which from the philosophical and theological perspective has become quasi-illiterate, we find the idea of God expressed in words as *something must exist*. In this context, can we ask ourselves who man is: the image of God? No. There is *something*, but we do not know much about it. Can we ask *something* questions? Be considerate of it? Have confidence in it? The ancient definition, which in the Aristotelian synthesis defines man as a rational animal, has been replaced by the definition of contemporary anthropology, which defines a human as a being capable of experience. But experience, as we all know, exists for a brief period in which we feel satisfied. In reality, all sorts of passions function this way. Will we therefore build marriage, the family, and the responsibility of a steadfast friendship on this anthropology?

We could continue this discussion endlessly. Surely we will hear ourselves say that today a human being is exposed to a continual assault of information and disinformation. This overload borders on psychological instability. Contemporary human life, which is growing longer, makes enormous demands on marriage and on the family. These institutions, after a certain time, exhaust the possibilities of surprise, experience, and pleasure, thus becoming boring and unattractive. This certainly explains many of the reasons for marital and family crises.

As for the biblical idea of man, the first pages of Sacred Scripture present to us someone who is described as the image of God. The fact that God is invisible, inconceivable, and inaccessible is never called into question on the pages of the Bible. They show that the encounter with God is a transformative event that cannot be forgotten. On the contrary, man, society, and the Israelites live by this event, which remains alive despite all catastrophes, even the Holocaust, and demonstrates its vitality. Moreover, this is true also of the new Israel, the Church. God defines himself when he answers the question "Who are you?" or "What is your name?" by saying: "I am who Am", "*Being*". He is not an impersonal being. We realize something that resounds within us, too. Even after seventy years of life, I carry within myself the permanence of *being*. I am precisely I and no one else. It takes only a moment of insomnia for the film of my life to be projected: all the wealth of experiences, surprises, joys, sometimes also disappointments and sorrows. But I ask: Can I become trite to myself? Certainly, there are moments in which I am disgusted. I am not only a man who seeks experiences; I am the being, the creature that thinks. Therefore I know that these are momentary emotions that end when the pain in my back ends, for example, or my headache. From biblical anthropology we know that the most essential thing that God declares to us is friendship, love. God professes his love for man.

Father, mother, the deepest relationships, the deepest feelings of which man is capable, are the image of Him-who-is, in other words, of the living, *being* God. Israel's prophets, unlike the ancient philosophers, define man as man who is capable of God (*homo capax Dei*). It is no accident that in the history of my nation [the Czech Republic], reading the prophets has always been a source, a wellspring in moments of the greatest humiliation, of occupation by totalitarian dictatorships, of persecution. Thus we discover what the negation of fatherhood and motherhood means in the subculture of contemporary society. Here we find the basis for the Church's warning, because she is convinced that father and mother are irreplaceable. Fatherhood and motherhood, as the mystery of the Triune God shows us, is the most profound richness of *Being*. During Passover, the Canticle of Canticles is read in the synagogue, the epitome of wedding songs, in which God is the bridegroom and Israel is the bride. This allegorical interpretation has not been studied sufficiently by Christian authors, but it is an authentic allegorical interpretation that became the reason for the inclusion of this poetic canticle in the canon of biblical books. Allow me to quote Rabbi Akiva: "If the Scriptures are sacred, the Canticle of Canticles is the most sacred."

The New Testament definition of God is: "God is love" (1 Jn 4:8). This is the definition of John, about whom the Gospel says that he was the disciple best loved by Jesus. This means that if I am the image of God, I am capable of loving. Love is the greatest wealth that one human being can give to another. If I want to speak about love for another, I must realize that I must be an active element that enters into that relationship. I cannot be merely someone who desires to be loved; this question is secondary, since the fact always remains that "God so loved the world . . ." (Jn 3:16). This priority of God's love commits man not to be satisfied with his own love but principally with making a gift of himself to the other. The current debasement of the word "love" shows that true love has been replaced by mere eroticism without the dimension of friendship and gift. It becomes something that we could compare to drug addiction, rather than the most profound manifestation of man.

Love cannot be the negation of freedom because it is not dependence but a free, deliberate decision *to be for the other and with the other*. Those who are in love endlessly desire and seek the answer to the question: "Do you love me?" and tell each other: "I love you!" In this way they express their free decision to form a relationship: thus the *covenant* is born, and they give each other *their word*. If we want to understand the crisis of the family and of marriage, we must ask what the term "word" means in today's society. The whole media and entertainment industry does not understand the *word* as an *event*, as self-communication, as giving oneself to the other, even though reciprocity, security, trust, and friendship are presupposed in human communication; rather, the media word becomes propaganda and publicity; it lies and seduces! For a long time now, it has not been enough to give one's word. I can say from personal experience that the thing I detest most is reading contracts, hundreds of pages that constantly seek to deceive. Today it seems that the word is no longer worth anything; it seems that only bondage [*l'obbligo*] has value. In the tradition of antiquity, one could be *obliged* or bound only to the devil, never to God. For God, a word is enough: "amen", "may it be so", "here I am", "I promise", "I give my word", or "I swear", because in reality this was an oath. This is the reason why God's covenants are concise, and therefore Jesus is content with just one commandment. Allow me to ask a question: What do we call a person who has not been faithful to his oath, who has not kept his given word, who does not remain at his post but flees like a coward? If we speak about the break-up of marriage, we have to realize that this is one of the most profound crises: it is not just a matter of the institution or of the violation of rules and laws, but of the *spouses' denial of each other and of who they themselves are*. And this is a betrayal.

At this point many of those who sorrowfully suffer the reality of a divorce that they did not cause will object that inhuman burdens are unjustly being imposed on them. But what do we expect of a soldier who ought to protect the post assigned to him, not to mention a household sheltering a mother with children? What should we expect, therefore, from a man or a woman who said, "I will never abandon you"? I do not deny the fact that there are situations the Church must seek to resolve, yet it is not possible to say that, generally speaking, man today is incapable of a firm, indissoluble tie. If we were to accept that statement, we would have to say that we are witnessing the most profound degradation of man in the history of humanity. God gave his word and kept it; he kept it on the Cross in Jesus Christ. Our debates about sacrifice and the legitimacy thereof are useless and sometimes completely irresponsible. The Cross is not the exaltation of torture, of killing. The Cross is the exaltation of faithful love. The Cross is the exaltation of keeping one's word, of the oath that God gave to mankind, of the God who trusts man. We must have great respect for those who have kept their word, and to them we express our profound gratitude. The crisis of the family includes within it the fundamental crisis of our whole society, which we can observe all around us. This crisis is simply part of the general anthropological crisis. In fidelity to the word of God, the synod will certainly consider how to help man, how to help the family, how to help marriage, so that it expresses the existential reality of our faith.

Finally, I would like to call attention to one thing: the synod should never forget the past and present scandal of the basic destruction of the word, of the promises of a large number of religious and priests in the latter half of the past century. We should realize that we are talking about the same, if not larger, scandal as the Inquisition and the other shortcomings, misunderstandings, and failings in Church history. A scandal that we must confess humbly in the presence of husbands and wives who, amid the thousand difficulties of their life in this era of degradation, are fighting to remain faithful to their promise, to their word, to the oath that they made to each other and to God.

Can Divorced and Civilly Remarried Persons Receive Communion?

Willem Jacobus Cardinal Eijk

In the last half century, one of the most heated debates in the Church has concerned the question of whether the divorced and civilly remarried can receive Eucharistic Communion. In a great many parishes in Western Europe, almost all these persons do receive it. Any priest who has the courage to be "mean" and to tell them that they are not properly disposed to receive can expect a very negative, emotional reaction. For the sake of the priests who are courageous enough to say so anyway, and also in the interest of the persons themselves who are involved, bishops have the obligation to bring clarity to this problematic situation from the doctrinal, theological, and pastoral perspective.

Doctrinal approach

In the 1970s, various theologians discussed this problem, without there being any precise pronouncement in this regard by the Magisterium of the Church. Nevertheless, there are *loci theologici* for this in Sacred Scripture and in the constant tradition of the Church that rule out the admission of the divorced and remarried to Holy Communion.

Jesus himself explicitly forbids repudiating one's wife and contracting another marriage and describes the latter as adultery (Mt 5:32; 19:9; Mk 10:11–12; Lk 16:18). Saint Paul declares that it is unlawful for either the husband or the wife to separate: "To the married I give charge, not I but the Lord, that the wife should not separate from her husband (but if she does, let her remain single or else be reconciled to her husband)— and that the husband should not divorce his wife" (1 Cor 7:10–11).

Willem Jacobus Cardinal Eijk is the archbishop of Utrecht.

The Eastern Orthodox Churches, which admit the possibility of a second and even of a third marriage of divorced persons, whereby they can receive Eucharistic Communion, see an argument for this practice in an exception that is supposedly found in the Gospel according to Matthew: "Whoever divorces his wife, except for unchastity (πορνία), and marries another, commits adultery" (Mt 19:9; cf. 5:32). However, does Matthew really allow an exception to the prohibition against divorce and remarriage for a married person whose spouse is guilty of "unchastity"? The question is: What is meant by the expression "unchastity" with which the Revised Standard Version of the Bible translates the Greek term πορνία (porneia)?

1. The meaning of the term πορνία is uncertain. It designates illicit sexual behavior, which may include adultery. We cannot jump to the conclusion that the term πορνία means adultery, because the Greek language has a word specifically for that: μοιχεία.

2. According to the classic Catholic solution, Matthew is not presenting a real exception because the verb απολύω does not refer to divorce in the sense of the dissolution of the marriage that would clear the way for a second marriage. The aforementioned verb refers instead to a separation from bed and the cessation of cohabitation without a second marriage in the case of an adulterous wife. In this interpretation, the clause "except for unchastity" would have to do with the separation from bed and would imply that this is lawful only in the case of a woman guilty of adultery.[1] We should note that the assumption that Jesus here is allowing a second marriage for the divorced person is based on an *argumentum ex silentio* [argument from silence]: in fact, Jesus does not say explicitly that it is lawful to contract a second marriage after a divorce.

3. It is most likely that πορνία here is a translation of the Hebrew term *zênût*, understood as an incestuous union within forbidden degrees of relationship (cf. Lev 18:6–18). In such a case there is in fact no marriage, and a decree of nullity would be required rather than a divorce. Therefore there is no obstacle to a marriage with another person. This use of the term πορνία is comparable to the use made by the Council of Jerusalem (around A.D. 50). The apostles, gathered in a council in Jerusalem, were answering the question of whether Christians of pagan origin must

---

[1] Saint Thomas Aquinas, *Super Evangelium S. Matthaei lectura*, 522 and 1559–60; cf. DH 1327.

follow the Jewish law: "It has seemed good to the Holy Spirit and to us to lay upon you no greater burden than these necessary things: that you abstain from what has been sacrificed to idols and from blood and from what is strangled and from unchastity" (Acts 15:28–29; cf. Lev 18:6–18).[2]

Given the uncertainties about the interpretation of the relevant passages in the Gospel of Matthew, the only sure way to proceed is as follows:

1. They must be interpreted in the light of the other pertinent passages in Sacred Scripture, which allow no exceptions to the indissolubility of marriage.
2. The authentic, definitive interpretation is up to the Magisterium of the Church.

Except for a few statements—which are not always formulated unambiguously—by some regional councils and various opinions of some Fathers of the Church that are not always consistent with those expressed elsewhere in their writings, the Catholic Church has forbidden divorce and remarriage in her official pronouncements from the fourth century on (Synod of Elvira [300–303]).[3] The Magisterium has always been clear and decisive about the indissolubility of a ratified and consummated marriage and about the absolute prohibition of divorce followed by a new marriage,[4] as is clear from the following list, which does not claim to be complete:

- Lateran Council III (1179);[5]
- Council of Trent (1563), canons 6 and 7 on marriage; canon 7 says that marriage cannot be dissolved, even by adultery committed by one of the spouses;[6]

[2] Cf. B. T. Viviano, "The Gospel according to Matthew", in *The New Jerome Biblical Commentary*, ed. Raymond Edward Brown, Joseph A. Fitzmyer, and Roland. E. Murphy (London: Bloomsbury Publishing, 2000), 643.

[3] DH 117.

[4] The idea that the Council of Nicaea (can. 8, DH 127) allows a second marriage after a divorce is based on a misinterpretation. Taken in context, this is a canon against the Novatians and therefore a rejection of their conviction that a second marriage after the death of a husband or of a wife was unlawful.

[5] DH 754–56.

[6] DH 1807.

- Pius VII, Brief *Etsi fraternitatis* (1803);[7]
- Leo XIII, Encyclical *Arcanum divinae* (1880);[8]
- Vatican Council II, Pastoral Constitution *Gaudium et spes*, 48;
- *Catechism of the Catholic Church*, nos. 2382, 2384, and 2385.

Contrary to the practice of the Eastern Orthodox Churches, which allow a second and even a third marriage for divorced persons, the Magisterium has always maintained the prohibition of divorce and remarriage, even for Eastern Rite Catholics (Council of Lyon II [1274],[9] Benedict XIV [1743][10]).

The moral object of a sexual relationship within the context of a civil marriage of a divorced and remarried person is ultimately a form of adultery, according to the above-cited words of Jesus himself. Seen in this light, the second civil "marriage" is not, in fact, another marriage, but a form of structured and institutionalized adultery. In 1803, Pius VII described the ratification of a second marriage after a divorce by pastors through their presence and their blessing as a "very serious crime" and a betrayal of their sacred ministry. These second marriages, Pius VII said, "should not be called nuptials, but rather adulterous unions".[11] According to a longstanding practice of the Church, those guilty of adultery in general cannot receive Eucharistic Communion. The Council of Trent describes adultery as a mortal sin through which the person involved loses the grace of justification already received[12] and is unworthy to receive Communion, unless he or she has repented of the sin, has confessed it, and no longer commits it.[13] From 1981 on, explicit statements that divorced and civilly remarried persons are not to be admitted to Communion have been made by Saint John Paul II (1981),[14]

---

[7] DH 2705–6.

[8] Leo XIII, *Arcanum divinae*, February 10, 1880, in *ASS* 12 (1879–1880): 385–402.

[9] DH 860.

[10] DH 2536.

[11] DH 2706.

[12] *Decree on Justification*, chap. 15, DH 1544.

[13] *Decree on the Sacrament of the Eucharist*, chap. 7, DH 1647. Cf. Paul's statement: "Whoever, therefore, eats the bread or drinks the cup of the Lord in an unworthy manner will be guilty of profaning the body and blood of the Lord. Let a man examine himself, and so eat of the bread and drink of the cup. For any one who eats and drinks without discerning the body eats and drinks judgment upon himself" (1 Cor 11:27–29).

[14] John Paul II, apostolic exhortation *Familiaris consortio* (November 22, 1981) (*FC*), 84.

by the Congregation for the Doctrine of the Faith (1994),[15] and by Benedict XVI (2012).[16] Saint John Paul II used the following language: "However, the Church reaffirms her practice, which is based upon Sacred Scripture, of not admitting to Eucharistic Communion divorced persons who have remarried."[17]

The Church's longstanding practice and repeated pronouncements of the Magisterium that a divorced and civilly remarried person cannot be admitted to Communion are standards indicating that this is an unchangeable doctrine.

Theological approach

In a report that it issued in 1977, the International Theological Commission says that the fundamental reason why it is impossible for the divorced and remarried to receive communion is the incompatibility of their state of life "with the precept and the mystery of the Paschal love of the Lord".[18] This is what Saint John Paul II affirmed in the apostolic exhortation *Familiaris consortio* (84).

There is a fundamental analogy between the relationship of Christ and the Church, on the one hand, and the relationship of two spouses, on the other, as indicated in the Letter to the Ephesians (5:23–32). The heart of the analogy is the fact that in both relationships the parties "mutually give and accept one another",[19] as stated in canon 1057 §2 (1983 CIC). In both cases, this gift is total, which also implies its definitive and therefore irrevocable character. The totality of the reciprocal gift of the spouses implies that it includes both the spiritual and the material dimension. Therefore, it is not a gift merely on the level of intention or emotion, but also encompasses the physical level, including sexual relations. We see here the importance of a correct, non-dualist

---

[15] Congregation for the Doctrine of the Faith, *Letter to the Bishops of the Catholic Church concerning the Reception of Holy Communion by the Divorced and Remarried Members of the Faithful* (September 4, 1995), 4.

[16] Benedict XVI, Pastoral Visit to the Archdiocese of Milan and 7th World Meeting of Families (June 1–3, 2012); Address during the Evening of Witness (June 2, 2012).

[17] FC 84.

[18] International Theological Commission, *Propositions on the Doctrine of Christian Marriage* (Rome, 1977), 5.3.

[19] In the documents of the Magisterium, the essence of marriage is described as a "mutual giving of self"; cf. Second Vatican Council, Pastoral Constitution on the Church in the Modern World, *Gaudium et spes* (December 7, 1965), 49.

anthropology that considers the physical dimension, too, as being intrinsic to the human person.

The Letter to the Ephesians adds that the love of the spouses is taken up into the charity of Christ himself, that is, into the reciprocal giving between him and the Church. The mutual gift between Christ and the Church is made present in the Eucharist, through which we share more intensely in this gift, that is, in his suffering, death, and Resurrection. Adultery—and therefore also a divorce followed by a new civil marriage—violates the totality of the reciprocal gift between spouses at the spiritual, emotional, and physical level and, consequently, is incompatible with the total, reciprocal gift between Christ and the Church, to which the gift of the spouses is analogous and into which it should be taken up. This is the fundamental reason why a divorced and remarried person cannot receive Communion.

We must realize that the question about administering Communion to divorced and civilly remarried persons is not an incidental, secondary matter. If we were to agree that it was, we would also be agreeing that the mutual gift of the spouses did not have to be total, either at the spiritual or at the physical level. Consequently, we would be compelled to change the Church's doctrine about marriage and sexuality in other areas. In this way we would weaken our essential arguments against adultery in general. The argument against the use of contraceptives is that their obstruction of the gift of maternity and the gift of paternity through the conjugal act makes the spouses' reciprocal gift and therefore the totality of the gift itself incomplete at the physical level (cf. *Familiaris consortio* 32). In abandoning the requirement of the totality and reciprocity of the gift, we would have to accept the use of contraceptives. If we were to agree that the reciprocal gift of the spouses did not have to be total and, therefore, that it was lawful to prevent the gift of a new life, we would be compelled to accept also sexual acts that are not directed to procreation at all, such as homosexual acts. The question of whether divorced and civilly remarried persons can receive Communion is intrinsically joined to other questions of marital and sexual morality.

Proposals for pastoral practice

More than a year ago, a Dutch journalist from a Catholic television station asked me why a divorced and remarried person must not receive Communion. I gave an answer based on the essence of marriage and of the Eucharist as described above. The journalist's reaction was typical of the present era: "Your Eminence, your answer is clear, but I am not sure I can explain it to my sister." Apparently he meant a divorced and remarried person. Since I do not know her, I do not dare to evaluate her capacity for understanding or her lack thereof. Nevertheless, there are two obvious possibilities: either his sister does not accept the Church's doctrine about marriage and the Eucharist, or she knows only that the Church forbids the divorced and remarried to receive Communion, without, however, really knowing the doctrine and, therefore, without understanding the reason behind the prohibition. The latter possibility is the more likely one in a country in which catechesis has been seriously neglected for half a century. In addition, there is the currently prevailing culture of pronounced individualism, which does not accept commonly held ideas or opinions, especially if they are thought to be imposed by an authority.

The solution to the problem of admitting the divorced and remarried to Eucharistic Communion is not primarily in speculating about a possible nullity of marriage because of a faulty knowledge of the faith or a lack of faith per se on the part of those who contracted it. Nor should we seek the solution in a simplification of the procedure for declaring nullity of marriage or in a special penitential process aimed at creating the possibility of receiving Communion without putting an end to the adulterous relationship. In his encyclical *Veritatis splendor*, Saint John Paul II refutes the misconception that pastoral practice consists of seeking to offer compromises between the Church's doctrine and complex everyday reality in the form of "so-called 'pastoral' solutions contrary to the teaching of the Magisterium" (56). True pastoral ministry means that the pastor leads the persons entrusted to his care to the truth definitively found in Jesus Christ, who is "the way, and the truth, and the life" (Jn 14:6). We must seek the solution to the lack of knowledge and understanding of the faith by transmitting and explaining its foundations more adequately and clearly than we have done in the last half century. The task that Christ has entrusted to us is, indeed, to proclaim the faith. In speaking about the foundations of the faith, we must realize that what has just been described is part of a broader problem. This problem touches on the essential content of the Church's doctrine on marriage and the Eucharist and also on the meaning of tradition and of the Magisterium. The Church by creating or at least tolerating confusion in this area at the same time creates or tolerates confusion with regard to fundamental questions of the faith. The problem of Communion for the divorced and remarried is therefore one part of a much larger problem.

Based on what has been said so far, it seems to me that it is important to consider the following proposals:

1. Every couple who present themselves for the sacrament of matrimony must receive thorough preparation, consisting of at least five or as many as ten meetings, which are to provide a clear and effective explanation of the central truths of the Church's doctrine, especially those truths regarding marriage and sexuality. There are good examples of these Christian marriage preparation courses in some ecclesiastical provinces and some new movements.

2. Whenever couples present themselves for a marriage in the Church, one should have the courage to ask them explicitly whether they accept the doctrine of the indissolubility of marriage. When the answer is uncertain or negative, it is necessary to dissuade them from marrying in the Church and, in their own interests, to be more selective in admitting such couples to the sacrament of matrimony. Otherwise, they run the risk of ending up in cohabitation and irregular relationships for which, often, it is not easy to find solutions in keeping with the Church's doctrine if their marriage fails and they divorce.

The purpose of these proposals is to prevent failed marriages. Another aspect is the pastoral care of divorced and civilly remarried couples. According to the Church's doctrine and longstanding practice in this regard, these persons cannot be admitted to Communion or to the sacrament of penance. Nonetheless, they should be invited to participate in the life of the Church and in her liturgical celebrations, to the extent possible within due limits. By using some creativity, ways should be found of assuring them that they are welcome in the Church. One classic bit of advice to persons who cannot receive Communion because of their state of life is generally to make a spiritual communion. The Congregation for the Doctrine of the Faith in 1994[20] and Benedict XVI

---

[20] Congregation for the Doctrine of the Faith, *Letter to the Bishops of the Catholic Church concerning the Reception of Holy Communion by the Divorced and Remarried Members of the Faithful* (September 14, 1995), 6.

in 2012[21] recommended this also for the divorced and remarried. This communion does not consist of receiving the Host, and therefore it is accomplished, not materially and corporeally, but rather spiritually by means of silent, interior prayer, with which the person expresses to Jesus faith in his Real Presence in the Eucharist and an ardent desire to receive it. One can make a spiritual communion during celebrations of the Eucharist by a mental prayer, while remaining at one's place, while the others go forward to receive sacramental Communion. However, even someone who is making only a spiritual communion could come forward with the others to receive a blessing instead of Communion. In Dutch dioceses, during Communion, while obviously allowing also the option of remaining at one's place and uniting oneself with Christ in silent prayer, all who want to are invited to come forward. Those who cannot receive Communion are asked to come forward with their arms crossed on the breast as a sign of the desire to receive a blessing. In this way it is possible to show all those who cannot receive sacramental Communion that they are welcome. This practice has proved to be an effective way of putting an end to heated, tiresome discussions about the fact that someone who is not in full communion with the Catholic Church, especially Protestants who are present at Eucharistic celebrations, cannot receive Holy Communion. The practice just described has dispelled the idea that they are excluded. The same can happen also in the case of divorced and civilly remarried persons. It is necessary to insist on the fact that spiritual communion and/or a blessing are also a source of grace.

One objection often raised is that a person who has the option of making a spiritual communion also has the right to receive sacramental Communion. This objection is based on the presumption that there is no difference between the two. Saint Thomas Aquinas explains this difference, making an analogy between baptism of desire and spiritual communion. The effect of the sacrament can be obtained by receiving it in desire, not in reality. Thus some individuals have been baptized with the baptism of desire. As we said earlier, spiritual communion consists of an ardent desire to receive the Eucharist. In an analogous sense, the effect of the Eucharist can also be obtained by means of a desire to receive this

---

[21] Benedict XVI, Pastoral Visit to the Archdiocese of Milan and 7th World Meeting of Families (June 1–3, 2012); Address during the Evening of Witness (June 2, 2012).

sacrament, although its effect is produced in a more complete way when it is actually received.[22]

Aside from the invitation to participate in liturgical celebrations to the limited extent possible, it is important to offer the divorced and remarried the pastoral care that is offered to all the faithful: personal pastoral accompaniment, the possibility of meetings and personal conversations, and the possibility of participating in the group activities of our parishes. The challenge for pastors is to show that the practice of the faith and participation in the life of the Church are not limited to Eucharistic Communion, although this is "the fount and apex of the whole Christian life".[23] Besides attendance at Eucharistic celebrations, making a spiritual communion, and receiving a special blessing at them, the divorced and remarried should be encouraged to read and listen to the Word of God, to practice *lectio divina*, to persevere in prayer, and to perform charitable works—things that ought to nourish and characterize every Christian's life anyway.

---

[22] Saint Thomas Aquinas, *Summa Theologiae*, III, q. 80, a. 1 ad 3.

[23] Second Vatican Council, Dogmatic Constitution on the Church, *Lumen gentium* (November 21, 1964), 11.

Marriage Preparation—The Challenges of Today

Joachim Cardinal Meisner

1. Status of affairs today: Marriage preparation?

In Germany, the responsibility for marriage preparation lies with the active clergy. At this time there are no standards set by the bishops' conference for the whole of Germany. Marriage preparation therefore is practiced very differently depending on the location. Not infrequently—I suspect this to be the rule in fact—preparation is reduced to filling out the marriage preparation forms and the liturgical planning of the wedding itself. There is no question about it: action needs to be taken.

Furthermore, I am convinced that a deep yearning for love without boundaries is rooted in the hearts of men. We are images of God, created out of love and for love. Man's greatest desire is the desire for love. And whoever has found love has found happiness.

In Cologne, a curious phenomenon has arisen. Directly behind the cathedral is an iron bridge across the Rhine River for pedestrians. Fixed to the grating between the railway and pedestrian crossing are hundreds of thousands of "love-locks". Couples go there to attach their locks to the bridge and then throw the key into the Rhine together. The lock represents their relationship, and they throw away the key in order to say: "We want to stay together forever." This is, of course, not a Christian ritual, but the essential elements of the marital relationship are expressed in a secular way within it: unity and indissolubility.

The message of our faith in the sacrament of matrimony is not foreign even to our secular world. It answers the deepest desire of men, and we say: "Your desire is no dream, no illusion, and no outlandish ideal.

Joachim Cardinal Meisner is the archbishop emeritus of Cologne.

Through Christ and his bond with the Church, love and fidelity are possible, wholly and without end."

Yet this message is overlaid with noisy and superficial messages that trivialize human relationships and especially sexuality and degrade them into cheap entertainment. As Pope Francis notes, relationships are included in the mentality of the "throwaway culture". Non-commitment and changeability take the place of fidelity and dependability. Our children grow up in this atmosphere and are influenced by the trivialization of relationships and sexuality in a profound way. Additionally, preaching about the truth, meaning, and sense of sexuality in Germany is practically nonexistent. Many of those in the Church responsible for evangelization shy away from talking about this "delicate subject". Not infrequently, priests and other Church employees are also confused about these issues. We also have to understand that many people have distanced themselves from the teaching and life of the Church.

Therefore, we can say that the situation of catechesis and faith with regard to the sacrament of matrimony in Germany poses a particular challenge. In light of this, I want to address a few aspects of marriage preparation.

2. Long-term preparation: What does "education to love" mean?

Marriage and celibacy are forms of life that involve the whole person, body and soul, together with all worldly dimensions. Both forms of life deal with love, which is more than a feeling, even more than well-wishing, but the basis of any friendship. They concern the climax of love, which is self-giving. Whoever gives himself not only gives something but becomes gift himself. Our ability actually to give ourselves is the fruit of the prior salvific gift of Jesus that finds its culmination in his Cross. "For even the Son of man also came not to be served but to serve, and to give his life as a ransom for many" (Mk 10:45), as the Lord himself explains his mission. The evening before his suffering, he gave his apostles the instruction to: "[l]ove one another as I have loved you" (Jn 15:12). Celibacy and marriage are totally different forms of life, but both follow, in their own way, this instruction of the Lord. Both forms of life imitate the love of Jesus.

We men are created out of love and for love. This gift of God becomes our mission. Love wants to be learned. Pope Saint John Paul II speaks about an "education for love" that is necessary for a proper unfolding of mankind.

Children in a family with several siblings learn what love is as a matter of course and quite naturally: knowing oneself to be sheltered in the love of parents, but at the same time realizing "in the end it is not my own will and wishes that are decisive; there are others as well." In this way, children learn to take responsibility for others in a family, to limit their own will, and to fit into a previously established community. At the same time, they learn dependability, responsibility, and fidelity—in short, attitudes and actions that are part of love or at least lead to it. Our day care centers have the important responsibility to support this "education for love" that is all the more necessary in the case of broken families.

Love and giving require the use of both body and soul. To come to know the dignity and meaning of love, the sense of sexuality and how to express it properly also belong to an "education for love". Our message is that sexuality is a great gift of God that serves to give love and to pass on life. In this context, Saint John Paul II speaks about the bridal meaning of the body. The body becomes a place and medium of self-giving both in celibacy and in married life.

The education for love that lies first and foremost with the parents requires intensive support by the Church's catechetical activity. The trivialization of sexuality has deeply penetrated Western civilization everywhere. From a very early stage, children are subject to its influence through the media and society. Even parents with good intentions often feel overwhelmed trying to counteract this social mainstream and are tempted to give in. And, unfortunately, the educational concepts of public schools do not always provide a reliable foundation for an education for love.

Part of the challenge of today's evangelization is to show youth the positive meaning of sexuality and relationships as well as to support parents in their duty to educate their offspring.

Marriage preparation is not limited to a few months before the wedding. It essentially begins with the education of young children. I am convinced that people themselves are our best "allies" in this regard. There is no greater desire in the hearts of men of all generations, of all nations, and of all races than to be loved and to love. Education for love in this context means showing modern man ways to the fulfillment of his deepest desire.

3. Short-term preparation: What is essential?

When we prepare a young couple for marriage, it is not to teach them something foreign, to place an excessive demand on their humanity. The idea is to help them unfold what they have inside, so that they—with the grace of God—can become the persons God intended them to be. Sometimes the image of God in men is covered with all kinds of rubble. Precisely because of this, engaged couples need our attention, our interest, our goodwill, and our affection. We do not do justice to engaged couples if we suspect that they want to marry only for the pleasures of an entirely secular celebration. If we do not truly accept them, we abandon them!

Affection and attention do not mean evading the truth of revelation or even hiding it. Rather, it is all about bringing to light the beauty and the truth of marriage and family. Pope Saint John Paul II's doctrinal teaching serves as a true gift here, especially his "Theology of the Body". He makes it clear that the teaching of the Church is a way to fulfillment and happiness, a way that is challenging but that will lead out of the constraints of egotism and consumerism into the "glorious liberty of the children of God" (Rom 8:21). In my view, this treasure is still far from having been unearthed yet. Without diminishing the Church's teaching, John Paul II was able to show that the Church's morality is no "wet-blanket morality", but is in fact a way to love and happiness. The apostolic exhortation *Familiaris consortio* of 1981 therefore remains a most helpful basis for marriage preparation. There are also a variety of courses of instruction on John Paul II's "Theology of the Body" that need to be advocated and promoted. Taking part in them is recommended for those who are in marriage preparation.

In my opinion, two important topics should not fail to be a part of any solid marriage preparation. First, there is the relation of love and fruitfulness. Blessed Paul VI has already shown the inseparability of these two aspects of sexuality in his prophetic encyclical *Humanae vitae*. The body is the voice of the soul, and, conversely, the soul is influenced by our bodiliness. The conjugal act is the highest act of love between man and woman. At the same time it is the act that, by will of the Creator, leads to new life. Love and fertility are two sides of the same coin. Those who in a manipulative way exclude fertility resist the creative will of God. At the same time, the human self-gift is destroyed. Whoever in a manipulative way excludes fertility tells his spouse: "I accept you, but not wholly: I do not accept your fertility."

Given the fact that many couples in our time have excluded fertility de facto by a variety of methods, we cannot remain silent about this. But experience also teaches that engaged couples—even those with a different style of life—are quite open to the Church's way of thinking. We must not leave them alone with theory. Many couples choose the way of "Natural Family Planning" (NFP). They are walking a path that respects the will of the Creator and lives parenthood in a responsible way. To guide them competently on this way—preferably with the help of experienced married couples—is necessary in marriage preparation.

The second topic that should not fail to be a part of marriage preparation is what John Paul II called the "language of love". The physical signs of love and affection should correspond to a spiritual love if they want to be genuine. The body has its own language that has been given to it. In this language, the conjugal act means a complete giving and surrendering of oneself to another. Sexual self-giving is consequently only truthful when it is incorporated into an offering of one's life and is the expression of that. Therefore, the only legitimate place for sexual communion is and remains marriage. There is no genuine love without truth.

Up to this point, even a non-Catholic or non-Christian can understand the topic of marriage preparation. The previously mentioned elements are universal human constants, truths rooted in the nature of man prior to any supernatural revelation. But the old saying is true: "Gratia supponit naturam"—"Grace builds on nature." This is especially clear in the sacrament of matrimony. Marriage is not a "new creation" of Christ, as are the other sacraments. Rather, the Lord takes up marriage as a reality of creation and inserts it into the order of redemption. Redemption with regard to marriage means that man and woman receive the capacity to love and to be faithful. Openness to offspring means not only a "yes" to creation but also a "yes" to redemption, since children, as baptized persons, are called to participate in Jesus Christ's work of redemption. Moreover, the bond of marriage is itself, beyond the union of the spouses, a sign of Christ's indissoluble bond with his Church. Therefore, marriage itself demonstrates Christ's work of redemption. The unbreakable fidelity of the spouses is a sign of the unbreakable fidelity of God.

In marriage preparation, it is important to show this connection, but also to make clear that this is a gift before it becomes a mission.

The sacrament of matrimony means that Christ enters as a third person into the union of two and gives this covenant a strength that would be impossible with human power alone. On this basis, the sacraments of confession and the Eucharist gain a special meaning as sacraments that nourish this bond and renew it.

4. What needs to be done?

With this in mind, what should characterize a priest, deacon, or another person in ecclesial office in order to ensure a good, timely, and practical marriage preparation? A solid preparation, a strong faith, and a good heart! What do we need to do in order to establish an engaging, truthful, reliable, and positive marriage preparation?

A. "Education for love" must become the pedagogical basis of our day care centers and schools. The first to receive this education are the children. Then it is a question of supporting parents in accord with their duty to educate their children.

B. The preparation of children for their First Communion in their understanding of the Real Presence of Christ in the Eucharist also includes the topic of self-giving: we live by the self-giving of Christ. We can love because he has first loved us.

C. Confirmation classes in Germany are taught to young people between the ages of fourteen and seventeen. Included in these lessons should be the recognition of the dignity of one's own body and its meaning. Learning to appreciate sexuality as a gift and a mission of God is a safeguard against trivialization.

D. There is an urgent need for a "framework for marriage preparation" for dioceses or, preferably, for the entire bishops' conference. In it the essential content for marriage preparation using a wide variety of permissible methodologies must be designated. It may be good to think about tying the observance of these general regulations to the formal validity of the church wedding.

E. "Natural Family Planning" is a way of responsible parenthood in accordance with the idea of sexuality prescribed by the Creator. NFP is not a method, but a form of life that presupposes mutual respect and the practice of the virtue of chastity. Respect and self-control are independently indispensable components of love. Informational materials, courses, and talks about these issues should be encouraged and disseminated.

F. In Germany the topic of marriage and sexual morality has only a marginal place, if that, in catechesis. Many Catholics have in their minds only a caricature of what the Church teaches. The Church is understood as a collection of rules and prohibitions that destroy fun and hurt love. Let us have the courage to proclaim the truth!

G. A subsequent challenge tied to marriage preparation is marriage accompaniment. What can we do in order to assist married people on their way of life, to remain with them in times of crisis, and to be with them should the marriage break down? How can we bring together couples of goodwill who can counsel one another? Marriage and family groups, retreat days, celebrations of wedding anniversaries, and similar activities can provide such occasions.

Marriage preparation and marriage accompaniment belong at the center of pastoral thinking today. Marriage and the family are the nucleus of Church and society. Not in vain does the enemy attack specifically here. I am thankful for the initiative of our Holy Father, Pope Francis, and my prayer goes out to him and the Synod Fathers, so that, guided by the Holy Spirit, they might bring the beauty and the truth of marriage and family to radiate anew.

Marriage in Our Contemporary World

Pastoral Observations from an African Perspective

John Cardinal Onaiyekan

Introduction

Today, marriage has become a matter for great debate both within and outside the Church. The debate has come even right into the sacred places of the Church of God, to the extent that a lot of our Christians are getting worried even to the point of panic. A good demonstration was what happened during the first session of the synod on the family, which took place in Rome in October 2014. Somewhere along the line, the mass media became full of rumors to the effect that finally the Catholic Church was changing her rigid position and was at last catching up with the rest of the world, not only in the reconsideration of divorce and remarriage, but also with regard to homosexuality and same-sex unions. I was not in Rome. I was in my house in Abuja. Phone calls were coming to me from both Nigeria and abroad from very concerned Catholics wondering what was happening to the Church. Interestingly enough, I receive calls from even non-Catholics, including Muslim friends, asking what was happening to our Church. My reply to them all was: "No need for panic. The boat of Peter may be in turbulence. But it will never sink. It will always arrive at its shores because Jesus is in it." We must have faith in the Holy Spirit guiding his Church. We must believe especially in the special grace of the Holy Spirit guiding the Vicar of Christ, the successor of Peter, our pope. I was glad and thrilled the next day to receive reports of the proceedings from the synod hall that went on to confirm my faith in the Church and that I passed on to those who a day before had reached out to me. We are in much the same situation

John Olorunfemi Cardinal Onaiyekan is the archbishop of Abuja, Nigeria.

today. It is a question of whether, indeed, there is such a thing as a doctrine of the Church that is firm, solid, and immutable or whether the Church will have to follow the latest developments and trends around us rather than lead humanity to salvation.

1. Contemporary developments

The issues of marriage and family should be placed within the general context of developments in the world of our day, especially in those societies that claim to be developed. Those societies also control the mass media, through which they almost succeed in misleading the rest of the world along the same line of error they have taken. Our modern world has made great strides in science and technology, with a lot of positive possibilities at the disposal of humanity. In fact, science and technology have reached the stage where the solutions to the great problems of the world, for example, hunger, disease, and even war and peace, are all within our reach. However, the same science and technology have evoked in the modern mentality, at least in some quarters, a sense of utter autonomy, the feeling that God and the spiritual do not matter. We do not need God. Humanity and nature are within the control of man himself. This is why we have many projects involving the total re-engineering of human nature.

It is in this context that we should place the tendency to see marriage in a completely different way from what humanity has been used to. This explains why homosexuality and same-sex unions are being vaunted as normal, perhaps even the preferred option. This is the world we have now around us, with its secularist approach to human society in total disregard for God, even if God is not being explicitly denied. Obviously, to this kind of environment, the Church does not matter. If God does not matter, how can the Church matter? We should, therefore, not be surprised that this so-called modern society completely rejects the position of the Church. Furthermore, while we try to engage in dialogue with this society, there is a limit to how much we can adjust our message to be acceptable. The Lord Jesus has already warned us that the world would prefer darkness to light.

2. The great apostasy

For a long time, all Christians had a common position on the main attributes of Christian marriage. Neither the great schism that gave rise to the Orthodox churches nor the Protestant Reformation that gave rise to the many Protestant churches tampered with the essential properties of marriage. All agreed that marriage is between a man and a woman, in unity and indissolubility. It is only recently that we have begun to see major shifts on the part of many Christian bodies. In the last couple of decades, it is as if a doctrinal earthquake had overtaken the Christian churches. It is difficult to explain the calamitous changes that have taken place without reference to the strong influence of the evil one. We must believe in diabolic forces; otherwise, a lot of things cannot be explained.

And so we have a situation where it seems that it is only the Catholic Church that continues to uphold marriage as a sacred institution from God and, indeed, as a sacrament into which we enter with a strong commitment to unity and indissolubility. We now see many around us claiming to be Christians and yet making provisions for polygamy and divorce in various forms. And, worst of all, they are approving the homosexual way of life to the extent of "blessing" the union between people of the same sex, which, they claim, is of equal status to marriage. It is bad enough when secular governments decide through their "democratic" processes to approve such aberrant situations. But the Church can live with that. What is more disgraceful, however, is that some Christian churches, in the name of the message of the Lord Jesus, have also given in to these aberrant positions. They have raised the homosexual way of life to the level of a normal Christian life-style. Lay Christians who are openly homosexual have been given full recognition and approbation. Even the clerical state, including the episcopacy, is now open to openly gay persons. And in all this, even the words of Scripture are not only reinterpreted, but simply laid aside in favor of the fait accompli.

The Catholic Church, however, thanks be to God, has up till now continued to maintain in her official doctrine that marriage is between one man and one woman and that once a marriage is validly celebrated, it is indissoluble. Of course the Church is aware of the difficulties of marriage and has designed pastoral ways of dealing with them. What we are now faced with is the fact that the errors mentioned above, which have eroded other Christian communities, are now invading our Church. Efforts to introduce changes in Church doctrine and practice are being persistently inflicted on our Church, not only by fringe theologians on the margins of the Church, but sometimes by people quite high up in the ecclesiastical realm. This is what we saw during the 2014 synod. We can only hope that the battle has now been laid to rest. It is important to realize that it is our faith that is at stake. The pressures out there are not likely to ease off, for the evil one has not surrendered.

3. Other religions today

In the face of the present confusion, it is ironic that the position taken by other religions seems to be even far more reasonable than that of some who claim to be Christians. Our experience has shown that the Muslim faith has remained firm on the fact that marriage is from God and that it has to be between a man and a woman. Of course Islam has always made provisions for both divorce and polygamy. But even those provisions are within the confines of Islamic law. While there are Muslims who are homosexuals, they have not gone to the point of raising homosexuality up to the level of a life-style to be promoted. From what we hear from other religions— Hinduism, Buddhism, and other religions in the East— they, too, have retained the basic understanding of marriage as a sacred institution to be handled with care and attention. They have also generally rejected the whole idea of homosexuality and same-sex marriage.

The order given to man by God to increase and multiply is reflected in the social life of humanity in every culture. That is why almost everywhere, there is recognition of the importance of the male and female sexes in the raising of families, reproduction, and the education of the next generation. Every culture has rules to guide this very important aspect of our human existence. Similarly, almost every culture has a clear conviction that this is not just a human affair but has sacred underpinnings. That is why marriage is often celebrated within the context of worship and ritual. Almost invariably, therefore, marriage and its consequences in terms of offspring and family are recognized as coming from God. This is surely what Jesus means when in Matthew he refers back to Genesis, saying: "In the beginning, it was not so" (Mt 19:18).

4. African traditional society

Let us now look specifically at the situation of marriage in our African traditional culture. My observations in this regard are meant to illustrate concretely the strong convictions of our people from their age-old traditions even before they were exposed to the Christian tradition.

We want to stress that in our own culture, marriage is clearly the *union of a man and a woman*. Homosexual behavior does exist but is always considered an abomination and punished as such. Therefore marriage is always between a man and a woman.

Marriage has also always been regarded *as sacred*. Before marriage, consultations are made through the instrument of divination. It is believed that God must be consulted to sanction the intention of a young man and woman to marry. There is also the belief that, along with God himself, the ancestors are involved in the process. All this stresses the fact that marriage is a sacred institution. Our people are therefore not surprised at the Christian doctrine of marriage as a sacrament, which they take squarely in their stride.

Also noteworthy in our concept of marriage is *the importance of offspring*. Marriage is meant especially for the continuation of the human species. The love of offspring in marriage is so strong that children are almost considered a necessary condition for the validity of marriage. A marriage without children is difficult to sustain. However, strictly speaking, it is not true to say that in African tradition, marriage without children is considered invalid. There are therefore no grounds for trying to promote any theological hypothesis aimed at making barrenness a ground for dissolution of a Catholic marriage in Africa, as some people have tried to suggest.

But what often happens is that when a marriage is childless, the man invariably seeks a second wife from whom he hopes to have children. Sometimes it is the barren wife herself who takes the initiative to bring another young girl into the family so that her husband will experience the fulfillment of children of his own. This reminds us of the story of Sarah and Abraham in the book of Genesis (Gen 16:1–3).

Sometimes too, because of barrenness, some women leave their husbands to try their luck with another man from whom they hope to have children. Sometimes they do begin to have children with another man. A possible scientific explanation for this could be that the first two people were genetically incompatible. Another example is when there is repeated infant mortality. Very often a woman leaves her husband for another man, and the children begin to survive. Today we may suspect that these were cases involving genotype incompatibility, a problem that is removed with a change of spouse. The same can happen when in a family the children are all girls and the man urgently needs a male heir who will take over the name of the family. Oftentimes the man will marry another woman simply for this reason.

All these cases underscore the importance of offspring in traditional African life. This is also an important element in the institution of marriage in the Christian faith.

It is often said that in Africa we practice *polygamy*. Often this is exaggerated. The most we can say is that polygamy is a respected form of marriage in many parts of Africa. That does not mean that every African male marries two or three wives. Demographically speaking, this would be impossible. There would not be enough women for every man to marry more than one, because the population of women is not two or three times that of men. Rather, polygamy is generally first and foremost the expression of affluence and status. Thus we find kings and chiefs acquiring many women as wives, resulting in large families. This in turn confers on them great respect in society.

It should be noted that in Africa, polygamy was never actually considered the norm, nor was it considered the ideal. In Yoruba culture, the Ifa Oracles are a compilation of the religious wisdom of the ancestors to guide the lives of the people. One of the texts in the *Eji Ogbe* chapter states:

> *Okan soso porogodo l'obinrin dun mo n'ile oko.*
> *Bi nwon di meji, won a d'ojowu.*
> *Bi won di meta, won a d'eta ntule.*

The translation is as follows:

> One and only one is the best number of women in a man's house.
> Make them two and they bring in jealousy.
> Make them three and they scatter your home.

This means that our people in their deepest spiritual values consider monogamy the ideal form of marriage.

As for divorce, there are provisions for it in the African traditional religion. Generally it is done with regret in cases where a marriage has broken down, sometimes through sheer incompatibility. At times the wife complains of being badly treated, and she decides to move somewhere else where she will receive better treatment. This does not mean, however, that the woman in Africa is a constant object of abuse. The normal scenario is that the woman is the respected mother in the family.

Sometimes, as already mentioned, divorce is a result of barrenness. In this case, it is only a last resort. This again affects Christian marriage.

5. Some challenges in Catholic marriage in Africa

On the whole, our people admire Catholic marriage. They wonder how it is possible to marry only one wife and stay with that wife for life. Of course we must constantly remind our members that Catholic marriage, one and indissoluble, is a sacrament in which God himself takes the initiative. It is therefore not through our strength that we are able to live successfully a marriage that is consistent and indissoluble.

A major challenge, frequent in the early era of evangelization in our lands, was what to do about *polygamists* who embrace the faith and seek to be admitted into the Church. The pastoral practice has always been to encourage their life of faith, including participation in the worship of the Church. But they have never been admitted to reception of Holy Communion unless and until they gave up their state of polygamy. This has meant choosing and keeping only one of the wives. This raises the question of what to do about the other women who cannot be simply thrown out of the house through no fault of their own. To devise a solution that respects the law of the Church as well as the demands of charity and even justice is often very difficult. Many, therefore, remain as they are, trusting in the mercy of God, without asking to receive Communion, regardless of their good intentions.

The considerations and interests mentioned in relation to marriage in traditional African society sometimes affect Catholic marriages. A major issue has to do with *offspring*. When a man is married in the Church and, after about ten years, is still without children, he is under great pressure from his family to marry another woman in order to have children. Very often in this case, the wife may not object and may even intervene in favor. Of course from the pastoral point of view, we do all we can to encourage people to sustain their marriage with or without offspring. Sometimes even the lack of a male child becomes a temptation to take another wife. This again is a constant concern in our pastoral care of marriages among Christians.

It is clear that our pastoral challenges are different from the situations we hear about in the so-called Christian lands. We hear that some people marry and do not want any children. Some even resort to abortion regularly when pregnancies occur. This should be a cause for great concern in the Church. We know that in our modern, globalized world, our own Christians in Africa are not totally free of the pressure from the so-called developed world to stop considering children to be a blessing from God. By and large, however, in the majority of cases, children are still very much considered a blessing from God. That does not exclude the need for responsible parenthood in the face of rampant poverty.

With regard to indissolubility, the desire for offspring has often created a special pastoral challenge for us even today with respect to *premarital sex*. Young couples know that they ought not to be living together and engaging in sexual activities before their wedding in the Church. However, in many situations, the couples already consider themselves married after the completion of the traditional marriage customs. The two families consider them married. It is very difficult to convince the young couple to refrain from sexual activities at that stage until the wedding has taken place in the Church. This is because of their strong desire for offspring. They firmly believe in the indissolubility of marriage once it is contracted in Church. They do not want to take the chance of entering into an indissoluble but barren marriage. Therefore, before they submit themselves to the commitment of marriage for life, both families want to ensure that both young people wanting to marry will be able to have children. And so even good Catholics often do not frown on this behavior and may sometimes even encourage the young couple to make sure that the betrothed wife is pregnant before they go to Church to make a lifelong commitment. In other words, even if today one can scientifically prove the possibility of offspring in a couple that intends to marry, the normal tendency is to prove this capacity first by means of a clear pregnancy and only then to enter into marriage in the Church.

Of course, there are couples who, out of respect for Catholic moral norms, refrain from sexual contact before their marriage in the Church. These are heroes we need to congratulate. After marriage some of them may encounter difficulties and be without a child for many years. With all the concomitant anxieties that accompany this situation, we need to pay special pastoral attention to such couples who are anxious for what they call "the fruit of the womb". Such pastoral care should not exclude adequate scientific and medical attention.

We know very well that our ideas about Catholic marriage are not shared by everybody around us. But we proudly uphold them as the ideal we have received from the Lord Jesus Christ. Christ has redeemed the whole world; and in the case of marriage, he has restored it to the level of a sacrament of faith. This has become a model for all, including those who may not be able to live up to its demands. This is where Catholic marriages and families can and must become the light of the world.

Conclusion

In conclusion, we should not forget the aim of the ongoing synod on marriage and the family. The synod has not been called to decide whether or not divorced and remarried couples can continue to receive Holy Communion. This is certainly not the purpose of the synod. Nor has the synod been called to discuss the issue of homosexuality and whether or not two Catholic men or two Catholic women can present themselves at the altar for marriage. That is not the purpose of the synod, nor indeed is it an issue in the Catholic Church. These are issues that are already clear in our doctrines. Synods are not called to change the doctrines or teachings of the Church. Rather, our synod has been called to confirm our faith, to study the pastoral challenges that face us, and to allow bishops to compare notes with each other so as to know how best to deal with these pastoral challenges. In this way, our people can be helped to live their Christian lives in marriage before God and as a witness before the entire community to the love, mercy, and fidelity of God himself to us. We hope that through the synod experience, the Catholic Church, through her pastors, with and under the successor of Peter, will emerge ever more powerful, vibrant, and vocal in proclaiming the truth of the Gospel of our Lord Jesus Christ. The more the world of our day is sunk down in immorality, the more there is need for the Church to be a light to the world for all to see. The model of Christian marriage is the Holy Family of Nazareth: Jesus, Mary, and Joseph. We place all our efforts under its patronage.

Witness to the Truth of the Gospel of the Family

An Urgent Pastoral Challenge for the Church to Set Out on the Journey of the Third Millennium

Antonio Maria Cardinal Rouco Varela

1. The convoking of two assemblies of the synod of bishops—one extraordinary, celebrated in the month of October of last year [2014], and the other ordinary, to be celebrated next October [2015]—is clear, unequivocal proof of the fact that our Holy Father, Pope Francis, judges and appreciates the seriousness of this historical moment, in which the Church of the twenty-first century finds herself faced with the challenge of proclaiming, celebrating, and serving the Gospel of the Family. This challenge can be taken up pastorally and apostolically in a fruitful way only if we realize that it is about welcoming an urgent call of the Spirit and about what he is asking of the Church today so that she can bring the love of her Lord and Bridegroom, Jesus Christ, "the Redeemer of man",[1] to mankind, which has already begun the new historical journey of the third millennium of Christianity. This welcome will be fruitful only if the Church, by her words and by her works, seriously takes into account the fact that "in a society thirsting for authentic human values and suffering from many divisions and fractures, the community of believers must be a bearer of the light of the Gospel, with the assurance that charity is, before all else, the communication of the truth."[2]

2. It is possible, or even probable, that the culture of the superficial and the provisional—to use the apt expression of Pope Francis—which envelops us like an invisible, inextricable social net, reaching even

---

Antonio Maria Cardinal Rouco Varela is the archbishop emeritus of Madrid.

[1] Saint John Paul II, encyclical *Redemptor hominis* (March 4, 1979).

[2] Benedict XVI, Address to the Participants in the Third Diocesan Synod of Madrid (July 3, 2005), *L'Osservatore Romano*, Spanish edition, July 8, 2005, no. 27.

into the most intimate aspects of personal life, might cause us to think that the great question about truth in everyday life—about how to know, affirm, and live it—is a minor matter that scarcely interests or concerns the younger generations. To lend pastoral credibility to this hypothesis would be a serious practical error that would reveal, moreover, a major deficiency: the lack of contact and of pastoral dealings with young people, carried out carefully with noble sincerity and with the discreet simplicity of someone who only wants their good, without ulterior or hidden motives. When this cordial communication with them is achieved, pastoral experience teaches again and again, in the most extraordinary and in the most ordinary situations in which one meets them—or they meet one another—inside or outside the ecclesial community, that the question concerning the truth about God, about man, about Jesus Christ, and about the Church affects them profoundly, not to mention when the question is asked with respect to the Church's doctrine about sexuality, marriage, and the family. This question is existentially dense and concrete. They want to know their truth! They want to know the truth! And we must not delude ourselves: to start pastorally from the pedagogical premise that the ideas originating in "gender ideology" have triumphed completely, overwhelmingly, and irreversibly, in theory and in practice, among our young people is to fail to know them in their deepest anxieties and personal yearnings and at the same time to fail to know how fragile and deceptive are the bits of meaning for the future of their lives offered to them by our contemporary society of pleasure and consumption at all costs and at any price. Yes, there is a crisis of the soul among the young people of our time! There is a crisis of love! They are aware of it and perceive it with a greater or lesser degree of sincerity when they are willing or obliged to acknowledge it. They are hiding it less and less! There is much evidence that can be inferred from the various, frequent sociological and psychological analyses that are so plentiful nowadays, promoted by many public and private institutions, which lead to the conclusion that our young people—today as always!—eagerly desire to find light: the light! The light of truth and the truth! In our frequent encounters with young people, individually or in groups, for the purpose of making a pastoral visitation of parish communities, centers of learning and of social services, at the university ... we detect with growing intensity this human and spiritual depth of the problems about which they are most worried and anxious, above and beyond the ones typical of persons their age, such as study, choosing a career, their professional future, engagement or "becoming a couple", to use a very common expression from the language of today's young people. Particularly noteworthy is the appreciation they have for the family as one of the values that most attract and convince them, although this appreciation does not of course keep them from living in a way that so flagrantly and so frequently contradicts it: for instance, such as embracing the life-style and the recreational and free-time habits that are so typical of them: sexually disordered habits that are personally devoid of true love. This shows, nevertheless, that we must not fear or waver when it comes time to proclaim to them the whole truth and the beauty of the Gospel of the Family. Although the appearances of their cultural world suggest otherwise, in the depths of their most intimate experiences they are hoping for it. Commenting on the diagnosis of Benedict XVI with respect to the form in which "the social question" is presented today, I would have to say that the question that arises in the life experience of the young person of our time in relation to sex and human love "has become a radically anthropological question": a problem that is "closely bound up with our understanding of the human soul".[3]

3. The truth of the Gospel of the Family, if set forth, celebrated, and served with fidelity to the Word of God, who creates and saves us, convinces and converts by its intellectual clarity and by the beauty of the "deeply" human aspect that it entails. Flowing from the infinite, merciful goodness of God's love for man, the truth of the Gospel of the Family clearly shows that the existential necessity of marriage as one, indissoluble, and fruitful, "the sanctuary of life and hope of society"[4] for the life of man and for the future of mankind, springs from the very truth about human love between a man and a woman. The sexual difference is a constitutive part of the human being as the image of God, called to be his child and, therefore, to participate in the Mystery of "God who is love": an irrevocable love! Or, to put it in other words, as the subject and historic recipient of love, in the saving plan of God the Creator and Redeemer, and called to participate in his glory. It would be fatal if, precisely while proclaiming and witnessing to the Gospel of

---

[3] Benedict XVI, encyclical *Caritas in veritate* (June 29, 2009), 75 and 76.

[4] Spanish Episcopal Conference, pastoral instruction *La Familia, Santuario de la Vida y Esperanza de la sociedad* (Madrid, 2001).

the Family and of marriage, its primordial feature and foundation, we were to forget to highlight the nature of man and the bodily and spiritual language in which he expresses himself. One of the main ethical and spiritual causes of the greatest tragedy suffered by mankind in all its history—World War II, which ended just seventy years ago—was no doubt the theoretical denial of the truth of the natural law, which was then put into practice relentlessly by oppressive political regimes that trampled on the dignity of the human person with ruthless cruelty, causing unprecedented levels of destruction and discrimination against man. A clear-sighted, courageous young university professor, Heinrich Rommen, ventured to publish in 1936, at the height of German National Socialism, a truly prophetic monograph about "the eternal return of the natural law". He wrote: "Actually, totalitarianism has only confirmed the remark by Saint Augustine: 'Without justice, what else is the State but a great band of robbers?' The natural law obliges all men and every individual."[5] In 1947, while the ruins of the war were still smoking, the second edition of his book appeared. It was a beacon light showing along what paths of moral and spiritual renewal the social, cultural, and political reconstruction of a new Europe would have to be directed.

Will it not be necessary to let the voice of nature be heard again, discerned in the light of the truth of the Creator, in these extraordinarily critical moments of a culture and of some social customs in which one of the most powerful and indispensable goods for the welfare of society and the happiness of persons, the family, founded upon true marital love, finds itself—at least in the countries of the Western world—at an authentic historical crossroads?[6] Only if we listen to this voice with intellectual honesty and interpret it consistently in our social and legal

---

[5] Heinrich Rommen, *Die ewige Wiederkehr des Naturrechts* (Leipzig, 1936; 2nd ed., Munich, 1947), 166: "Der Totalitarismus hat eigentlich nur des heiligen Augustinus Wort: 'Ohne Gerechtigkeit, was sind die Staaten anderes als grosse Räuberbanden,' aufs neue bestätigt. Das Naturrecht verpflichtet alle Menschen und jeden Einzelnen."

[6] Pope Francis, apostolic exhortation *Evangelii gaudium* (November 24, 2013) (*EG*), 66 and 67: "The family is experiencing a profound cultural crisis, as are all communities and social bonds. In the case of the family, the weakening of these bonds is particularly serious because the family is the fundamental cell of society, where we learn to live with others despite our differences and to belong to one another; it is also the place where parents pass on the faith to their children.... The individualism of our postmodern and globalized era favors a lifestyle which weakens the development and stability of personal relationships and distorts family bonds."

practice will we be able to get out of this tragic situation characterized by the massive, radical questioning of marriage as an indissoluble community of love between one man and one woman that is open to the gift of life and from which the family emerges.[7] Nothing is more existentially necessary or more historically urgent than to return to an acknowledgment of the natural law that founds, supports, and orders marriage, above and beyond any historical constellation of factors. Marriage and the family are not a mere product of human power—of any human power whatsoever, in particular that of the political authority—that can control or manipulate it at its whim. On the contrary, its being and essential design are those of a natural institution, ordained and willed by God. Luther, who denied the sacramental character of marriage, nevertheless acknowledged that it was instituted by God: "institutum a Deo". Marriage and the family are realities inherent in human nature before the State is, and they are so to an extent that is even more basic and fundamental than the political community.[8] It is important to insist again that the Church's pastoral action is more fruitful, the more she proves capable of awakening and quenching in the young people of today, who are the victims of so many broken marriages and families, the thirst for existential authenticity that is so typical of youth that there is no other way to satisfy it except by being able to see and grasp the vocation to true, authentic love as it is inscribed in the innermost personal being: the love of husband and wife.[9] At the very heart of the noisy musical culture that surrounds and fascinates them, it is not difficult to discover, at the same time, nostalgia and longing for authenticity in their lives and for authenticity in love: the ardent desire to live the truth in their love! The truth of human love as opposed to all the passions stirred up by the classic enemies of the soul: the devil, the world, and the flesh!

[7] Second Vatican Council, Pastoral Constitution on the Church in the Modern World, *Gaudium et spes* (December 7, 1965), 48: "The intimate partnership of married life and love has been established by the Creator and qualified by His laws.... As a mutual gift of two persons, this intimate union and the good of the children impose total fidelity on the spouses and argue for an unbreakable oneness between them."

[8] Antonio Maria Rouco Varela, "Peculiaridad cristiana del matrimonio entre cristianos de distintas Iglesias", *Diálogo Ecuménico* 29 (1973): 203–27.

[9] The concept of "one's existential ends" is very thought-provoking and helps us to understand the close relationship between the theory and the experience of the natural law; the concept was explained and set forth in a masterly way by Johannes Messner, *Das Naturrecht* (Innsbruck, Vienna, and Munich, 1960), 40–45.

4. The experience of living fully the natural truth of marriage and of the family runs into an apparently insurmountable obstacle: that of a nature wounded by original sin and its consequences—in a word, with the obstacle of "fallen nature". Man can be deceived and bewildered in his reason, seduced and attracted in his heart to make room in his life for thoughts, words, and deeds that he would rather keep at a distance from his will, although it seems to him that he cannot do so. His experience of freedom may turn, on many occasions, into an experience of humiliating external and internal slavery. This center, the innermost part of the human being—his heart!—in which is rooted his primordial vocation to mutual self-giving between a man and a woman, spiritually and corporeally, is precisely where the effects of original sin work most virulently. There is nothing strange about that, since we are talking about an unconditional gift forever, which is consummated in matrimony and is naturally fruitful in the gift of children—children who are procreated and not produced[10]—something diametrically opposed to what the sin of Adam and Eve signified! Consequently, it is not surprising that this "sanctuary" of the human person was the place where those who deny the soul and reject the Spirit penetrated most destructively over the course of the history of mankind, of its civilization and cultures. The power of their existential fascination is insidious; neither could the People of the Old Covenant, whom God had elected and guided by his commandments, escape from it. This fascination has been extraordinarily disturbing and lethal in its moral and religious consequences and has often obstructed their journey through salvation history. Some Pharisees approached Jesus himself "and tested him by asking, 'Is it lawful to divorce one's wife for any cause?' He answered, 'Have you not read that he who made them from the beginning made them male and female, and said, "For this reason a man shall leave his father and mother and be joined to his wife, and the two shall become one"? So they are no longer two but one. What therefore God has joined together, let no man put asunder.'" When they persisted with

---

[10] The expression comes from the writings of Olegario González de Cardedal, who used it, above all, as a category very rich in meaning for the understanding of Christianity in its more specific aspects. Cf. Olegario González de Cardedal, *La Entraña del Cristianismo* (Salamanca, 1997), 43–59, 72. See Juan A. Martínez Camino, *¿Qué pasa por fabricar hombres? Clonación, reproducción artificial y antropología cristiana* (Bilbao, 2000), 71, 72; and Eberhard Schockenhoff, *Ethik des Lebens: Ein Theologischer Grundriss*, 2nd ed. (Mainz, 1998).

their argument, demanding an explanation for why Moses commanded that a man give his wife a certificate of divorce and put her away, he replied: " 'For your hardness of heart Moses allowed you to divorce your wives, but from the beginning it was not so' " (Mt 19:3–9). Who would dare to deny that hardness of heart continued to be at work afterward in the new course of salvation history, that is, during the definitive chapter of the People of the New Covenant? And therefore, who would not consider himself obliged to admit that it has taken hold of and continues to take hold of the conscience of many of our contemporaries, including our brethren in the faith, grown-ups and adolescents, and of course ourselves? "Hardness of heart" has existed, exists, and will continue to exist with greater or lesser intensity and seriousness in "the time of the Church": today as formerly! The history of canonical marriage law shows clearly and emblematically: "It is not surprising—the masters of this modern branch of historical science assert—that the history of the canonical system of marriage has been considered a battle for indissolubility."[11]

5. However, the hardness of our hearts has been conquered by the greater gift of love that we have received from God through the Incarnation and the Paschal Mystery of his Son, Jesus Christ; by suffering and dying on a Cross for us and by rising again for our salvation, he redeemed us from sin and death and through the grace of the Holy Spirit has given us a new heart. The mystery of an infinitely merciful love! "As the Father has loved me, so have I loved you; abide in my love" (Jn 15:9). Since we have been introduced undeservedly into the ineffable Mystery of a God whose love forgives his creature, man (man and woman), and who, moreover, wishes to make them his children in his only begotten Son, Jesus, so much so that he gave him up to death, even death on the Cross, what he asks of us is simple, sublime, and joyful: to abide in his love! This commandment of the Lord applies very especially to Christian marriages and to the young people who want to contract it. And the love of Jesus is great, unfathomable, and, at the same time, close and tender. He calls his disciples "friends", and, together with them, that includes us (an "us" that many times includes those who are bereft of human love) and also the young people in

[11] Cf. Nicolás Alvarez de las Asturias, *En la Salud y en la enfermedad: Pastoral y Derecho al servicio del matrimonio* (Madrid, 2015), 69.

the present hour of the Church and of mankind—friends for whom he gave his life: "Greater love has no man than this, that a man lay down his life for his friends" (Jn 15:13). He no longer calls us servants, because a servant does not know what his master is doing. As he said to his first disciples at the first hour, he says to us: "I have called you friends, for all that I have heard from my Father I have made known to you" (Jn 15:15). He granted to us to know the truth about marriage and the family in all its original beauty, as the Father planned it, and, at the same time, he granted us the grace to be able to live it with the strength and in the presence of his own love, so much so that he transforms the love of the husband for the wife and of the wife for the husband into a living and efficacious sign of his love for the Church, purchased by his Blood, which was poured out on the Cross for all mankind, thus making her his Bride. In the Church, who is Bride and Mother, Christian spouses find the place and the time where their spousal love can flourish unto eternity. Already in his family, with Mary and Joseph, his parents, "the Holy Family of Nazareth", Jesus began and brought to its culmination the definitive plan of God's saving love for mankind (Mary was with him at the foot of the Cross), setting before us the model of the Christian family. Everything is pure love in the virginal Yes of Mary to the Angel's announcement that she was to conceive the Son of God by the work of the Holy Spirit. Her maternity is a motherhood that is—all of it!—love alone; love in its root and in its actualization. It is also, definitely, virginal love that inspires and works in the Yes of Joseph, who is willing to take his betrothed, the Virgin Mary, into his home after the revelation by the Angel (cf. Mt 1:20). This is the Yes of the first Christian husband: the model Yes. The spiritual fruitfulness of this family would be unlimited: it went on to reach all the ends of the earth and to last until the end of time! Then, the presence of Jesus at the wedding feast of Cana in Galilee, when he changed water into good wine for the banquet, granting the request of his Mother, reveals touchingly that this presence will never fail Christian marriage, with the same effects as those that it produced in the spouses at the wedding that his Mother was attending and to which Jesus and his disciples had been invited (cf. Jn 2:1–12). By his sacramental presence at the weddings of those who celebrate in his Church their human love (the water), through the power of his divine love, that love will be healed, elevated, and transformed into "the good wine" of the love of his Sacred Heart. From the Cross this presence will be sacramentally confirmed forever.[12]

6. The entire pastoral ministry of the Church with respect to the Gospel of the Family is worthy of that name when it takes place and results in the close accompaniment of her young people through the spiritual process of overcoming the experience of hardness of heart, changing it into the experience of the real and realized possibility of a new heart, touched and transformed by the love of the Heart of Christ. This process will gel—it will have results in their lives!—if it follows a pastoral path in which the word of faith and the celebration of its mysteries in the liturgy foster the creation of an atmosphere of ecclesial communication imbued with "communion", in which human love, inflamed in the noble and pure agreement between the young man and the young woman, begins to be understood and lived as a deep vocation to a true, authentic love, which is destined to be joyously fruitful in the new lives of the children, in a word, in the family: "the domestic Church", a community of life and love, without which men lose the capacity to be and to live in community as "friends" in any area of human coexistence. This is a word that means much more—qualitatively more!—than simply and coldly being "partners".[13]

Yes, this pastoral care of marriage and the family is possible. Furthermore, it is in fact spreading; it can be observed and is currently doing productive work in old Europe in not a few parish communities, in various and varied movements and ecclesial communities, and in valuable and valiant initiatives for the pro-life cause and for the truth of marriage and the family that are carried out in the field of civil society and the political community, not infrequently combining forces with non-believing fellow citizens who are nevertheless very sensitive to the value of what is at stake. It is, with everything else in the human and spiritual context of ecclesial welcome that is inspired by fraternal charity, the place where marriages and families in crisis, separated and divorced persons, find the open door of the authentic, integral faith and the living experience that clarifies for them the vital prospect in which the full

---

[12]John Paul II, apostolic exhortation *Familiaris consortio* (November 22, 1981), 12; Benedict XVI, post-synodal apostolic exhortation *Sacramentum caritatis* (February 22, 2007), 27–29; Pope Francis, encyclical *Lumen fidei* (June 29, 2013) (*LF*), 5; cf. Antonio Maria Rouco Varela, *La Familia, motivo de esperanza* (Madrid, 2015), 89ff.

[13]Cf. Ferdinand Tönnies, *Gemeinschaft und Gesellschaft* (Leipzig, 1885).

truth of Christian love can be actualized and put into practice in marital and family life without any decrease, either of its theological content or of its canonical-ecclesial form of life. Yes, if an atmosphere is created in which the experience of the "personal encounter with the saving love of Jesus"—about which the Holy Father, Pope Francis, speaks to us so beautifully in *Evangelii gaudium*—is made possible humanly and spiritually, ecclesially and pastorally, then the truth of the Gospel of the Family is and will become a living, vivid reality without any curtailment or compromise. Because it is possible to verify precisely in the field of marital and family life "how much good it does us when he once more touches our lives and impels us to share his new life", not only in more fortunate circumstances, but, above all, in the most distressing times of marriage and of the Christian family. Because "what then happens is that 'we speak of what we have seen and heard' (1 Jn 1:3)."[14] In this way, by sharing the experiences and the prayer of married couples and of Christian families within the ecclesial community, spousal love and the love of the family become "missionary". The Church in Europe (and throughout the world) urgently needs missionary families—families on a mission! This is an urgent need with few parallels in past centuries! "Those who have opened their hearts to God's love, heard his voice, and received his light cannot keep this gift to themselves", Pope Francis teaches in his encyclical letter *Lumen fidei*. This is perhaps the deepest, most essential dimension of what the Christian family is and what it is called to be today! And "since faith is hearing and seeing [and] is also handed on as word and light",[15] so it has to happen with the transmission of the faith by Christian families, above all, in relation to the dimension of the gospel that affects them so directly and essentially: the Gospel of the Family! It is entirely up to them whether or not the witness to this gospel—the gospel of marriage and of the Christian family!—resounds and shines forth in the Church and throughout society in our day in all its luminous, authentic truth! In order to achieve this, they must not forget to commend themselves to the Holy Family of Nazareth: to Jesus, Mary, and Joseph.

[14] *EG* 264.
[15] *LF* 37.

The Gospel of the Family in the Secularized West

Camillo Cardinal Ruini

That fundamental cell of society which is the family is going through a period of extraordinarily rapid evolution. Premarital relationships are now lived out in the open, and divorce is almost normal, often as a result of the breaking of conjugal fidelity. This is pulling us away from the traditional physiognomy of the family in countries and cultures marked by Christianity. In recent decades, moreover, at least in the West, we have entered into unexplored territory. Inroads have been made, in fact, by the ideas of "gender" and of "homosexual marriage". At the root of all of this is the primacy, and almost the absolutization, of individual freedom and of personal sentiment. So the family bond must be capable of being molded at will, and in any case not binding, to the point of disappearing or becoming practically irrelevant. According to the same logic, this bond must be accessible to every kind of couple, on the basis of the assertion of a complete equality that admits no differences, above all those that can be attributed to an external will, whether this be human (civil laws) or divine (the natural law).

The desire to have a family and if possible a stable family, however, remains strong and widespread: a desire that is translated into the reality of many "normal" families and also numerous authentically Christian families. These last are certainly a minority, but they are substantial and strongly motivated. The sense that the family, properly understood, is disappearing is therefore to a large extent the result of the distance between the real world and the virtual world constructed by the media, although it must not be forgotten that this virtual world has a powerful influence on real behavior.

Carlo Cardinal Ruini is the vicar general emeritus of His Holiness for the Diocese of Rome.

In a serene and balanced view, therefore, there seems to be little foundation for unilateral pessimism and resignation with regard to the family and its future. What the pastoral care of the family needs instead is the attitude of the Second Vatican Council toward the new times, an attitude that we can summarize as a spirit of welcome that redirects everything toward Christ the Savior.

In concrete terms, with the Second Vatican Council's Pastoral Constitution on the Church in the Modern World, known also by its Latin title, *Gaudium et spes*, we have a new approach to marriage and the family (47–52), more personalistic but with no rupture from the traditional conception. Following this document, Saint John Paul II offered the Church a catechesis on human love that, along with his apostolic exhortation *Familiaris consortio* of 1981, constituted a tremendous exploration that opened new perspectives and confronted many current problems in marriage and family life. Although these catecheses could not deal explicitly with more recent and more radical developments, like gender theory and same-sex marriage, they already laid the foundations, to a large extent, for addressing them. Without a doubt, pastoral practice has not always lived up to these teachings—besides, it could never do so completely—but it has followed their guidelines with important results: our young Christian families, in fact, are also the fruit of these.

The synods on the family

Now, with Pope Francis, we have already had a synod on the pastoral challenges of the family in the context of the new evangelization, and we are about to have another one: a further step in this journey of welcoming and reorientation that the whole Church is called to undertake with trust.

The perspective of the synod must be clearly universal, and no geographical or cultural area can demand that the synod concentrate only on its own problems. Having established that, the most significant questions for the West seem to be the more radical ones that have emerged in recent decades. These urge us to rethink and to present anew, in the light of the Gospel of the Family, the meaning and value of marriage as a covenant of life between man and woman, oriented to the good of both and to the procreation and education of children, and endowed with a decisive social and public significance as well. Here the Christian faith must demonstrate true cultural creativity, something that the synods are not able to produce automatically but can stimulate in believers and in those who realize that what is at stake is a fundamental human dimension.

Divorced and civilly remarried Catholics

But there are other questions that continue to confront us and seem to become ever more urgent, already repeatedly addressed by the Magisterium. Among these is that of the divorced and civilly remarried. Saint John Paul II's apostolic exhortation *Familiaris consortio* (84) has already indicated the attitude we should adopt: not to abandon those who find themselves in this situation, but, on the contrary, to take special care of them, striving to make the Church's means of salvation available to them. This means helping them, not to consider themselves separate from the Church by any means, but instead to participate in her life. It also means carefully discerning the situations, especially those of unjustly abandoned spouses as opposed to those who have culpably destroyed their own marriage.

Familiaris consortio, however, also reiterates the practice of the Church, "which is based upon Sacred Scripture, of not admitting to Eucharistic Communion divorced persons who have remarried". The fundamental reason is that "their state and condition of life objectively contradict that union of love between Christ and the Church which is signified and effected by the Eucharist." What is in question is, therefore, not their personal blame, but the state in which they objectively find themselves. This is why a man and woman who for serious reasons, like, for example, the raising of children, cannot satisfy the obligation of separation in order to receive sacramental absolution and the Eucharist must take on "the duty to live in complete continence, that is, by abstinence from the acts proper to married couples" (84).

This is undoubtedly a very difficult commitment, which is taken on by very few couples, while the divorced and remarried are unfortunately ever more numerous. A search for other solutions has therefore been underway for some time. One of these, while holding firm the indissolubility of ratified and consummated marriage, maintains that the divorced and civilly remarried could be allowed to receive sacramental absolution and the Eucharist under precise conditions but without having to abstain from the acts proper to spouses. This would amount to a second table of salvation, offered on the basis of the criterion of *epikeia* in an effort to unite truth and mercy. However, this way does not seem viable mainly because it implies an exercise of extra-marital sexuality, given the continuation of the first marriage, ratified and consummated. In other words, the original conjugal bond would continue to exist, but in the behavior of the faithful and in liturgical life, one could proceed as if it did not exist. We are therefore facing a question of consistency between practice and doctrine, and not only a disciplinary problem. As for canonical *epikeia* and *aequitas*, these are very important criteria in the area of human and purely ecclesial norms, but they cannot be applied to the norms of divine law, over which the Church has no discretional power.

This does not mean that every possibility of development is precluded. One way that appears viable is that of revising the processes of nullifying marriages: these are in fact norms of ecclesial law, not divine. There must, therefore, be an examination of the possibility of replacing the judicial process with an administrative and pastoral procedure, essentially aimed at clarifying the situation of the couple before God and the Church. It is very important, however, that any change of procedure must not become a pretext for granting in a surreptitious manner what in reality would be divorces: hypocrisy of this nature would bring great harm to the whole Church.

Faith and sacramental marriages

One question that goes beyond the procedural aspects is that of the relationship between the faith of those who marry and the sacrament of marriage. *Familiaris consortio*, no. 68, rightly places the accent on the reasons that induce one to maintain that those asking for canonical marriage have faith, albeit in a weakened condition that must be rediscovered, strengthened, and matured. It also emphasizes that social reasons can licitly enter into the request for this form of marriage. It is therefore sufficient that the engaged couple "at least implicitly consent to what the Church intends to do when she celebrates marriage". The attempt to establish further criteria of admission to the celebration, which would take into account the level of faith on the part of those to be married, would instead involve grave risks, starting with that of pronouncing unfounded and discriminatory judgments.

In fact, however, there are unfortunately many baptized today who have never believed or no longer believe in God. This therefore raises the question of whether they can validly contract a sacramental marriage. On this point, Cardinal Ratzinger's introduction to the booklet *On the Pastoral Care of the Divorced and Remarried*, published in 1998 by the Congregation for the Doctrine of the Faith, retains its fundamental value.[1]

Ratzinger maintains that it must be clarified "whether every marriage between two baptized persons is *ipso facto* a sacramental marriage".[2] The Code of Canon Law affirms this (can. 1055 §2), but, as Ratzinger observes, the Code itself says that this applies to a valid marriage contract, and in this case it is precisely the validity that is in question. Ratzinger adds: "Faith belongs to the essence of the sacrament; what remains to be clarified is the juridical question of what evidence of the 'absence of faith' would have as a consequence that the sacrament does not come into being."

It therefore seems to have been established that if there truly is no faith, neither is there the sacrament of matrimony. With regard to implicit faith, the scholastic tradition, with reference to Hebrews 11:6 ("whoever who would draw near to God must believe that he exists and that he rewards those who seek him"), requires at least faith in God as recompensor and savior. It seems to me, however, that this tradition must be updated in the light of the teaching of Vatican II, on the basis of which the salvation that requires faith can also be obtained by "all men of good will in whose hearts grace works in an unseen way", including those who maintain that they are atheists or in any case have not come to an explicit knowledge of God (cf. *Gaudium et spes* 22; *Lumen gentium* 16). In any event, this teaching of the Council by no means implies an automatism of salvation and a trivialization of the need for faith: it instead places the accent, not on an abstract intellectual recognition of God, but rather on an adherence, however implicit, to him as the fundamental choice of our life. In the light of this criterion, it could perhaps be maintained that under the current circumstances there are more baptized persons who do not have faith and, therefore, cannot validly contract sacramental marriage.

[1] Congregation for the Doctrine of the Faith, *Sulla pastorale dei divorziati* (Vatican City: Libreria Editrice Vaticana, 1998), 7–29.
[2] Ibid., 27–28.

It therefore seems truly opportune and urgent to strive to clarify the juridical question of that "evidence of lack of faith" which would make sacramental marriages invalid and prevent nonbelieving baptized persons from contracting such marriages in the future. We must not conceal the fact, on the other hand, that this opens the way for much more profound and difficult changes, not only for the Church's pastoral care, but also for the situation of nonbelieving baptized persons. It is clear, in fact, that, like every person, they have the right to marriage, which they would contract in civil form. The greatest difficulty does not lie in the danger of compromising the relationship between the canonical order and the civil order: their synergy has already become very weak and problematic through the progressive distancing of civil marriage from the essential requisites of natural marriage itself. The effort of Christians and of those who are aware of the human and social importance of the family founded on marriage should instead be aimed at helping the men and women of today to rediscover the significance of those requisites. They are founded on the order of creation and precisely for this reason apply to every age and can be made concrete in forms adapted to the most diverse times.

I would like to end by recalling the common intention that animates those who are taking part in the synodal debate: to hold together, in pastoral care for the family, the truth of God and of man with the merciful love of God for us, which is the heart of the Gospel.

Marriage Preparation in a Secularized World

Robert Cardinal Sarah

How could marriage preparation programs address more effectively the situation of poorly catechized young couples who are heavily influenced by a secularist culture?

"Take away the supernatural, and what remains is the unnatural", said the British author G. K. Chesterton. Cut off from God, human love does not remain human for long. In secularized Western society, the extent of the distress reveals the depth of the wound inflicted on truth and on human happiness. Laws about homosexual unions are contrary even to common sense, and statistics on divorce (in certain major cities, one out of every two marriages ends in separation) reveal a veritable "plague"[1] and show the fragility of any commitment. As for the way marriage or human love is depicted in art or merely in the media, the images are often one-sided and sometimes hopeless or degrading.

If Christ alone reveals the truth about man, then in rejecting him we lose the meaning of human nature. Sin mars the face of man. Now Christ came not only to save us, but also to repair what sin has broken, to snatch man away from all that disfigures him, so as to restore to human destiny all its breadth and fullness.

Marriage preparation must take up this challenge. The Church, especially in countries with a secularized culture, must perform an urgent work of evangelization. Certainly, in Africa and Asia human love in its

Robert Cardinal Sarah, formerly archbishop of Conakry, Guinea (1979–2001), secretary of the Congregation for the Evangelization of Peoples (2001–2010), and president of the Pontifical Council *Cor unum* (2010–2014), is currently prefect of the Congregation for Divine Worship and the Discipline of the Sacraments.

[1] Second Vatican Council, Pastoral Constitution on the Church in the Modern World, *Gaudium et spes* (December 7, 1965) (GS), 47.

natural dimension is less degraded than in the West. Nevertheless, even there, pressure from international lobbies and the media make it a burning issue that pastors are obliged to address.

IGNORANCE OF HUMAN LOVE AND INSTRUCTION IN THE FAITH: THE TEACHING OF VATICAN II

Restoring authentic human love

In Western countries most young people who ask to be married are already cohabiting, and there are many who already have a child. One might be tempted to think that these experiences have given them human maturity and that the work of preparation would be reduced to an exploration of the sacrament.

From this perspective, people often recommend "meeting the fiancés where they are". If by that they mean that the cohabiting partners already experience a natural conjugal love and that there is nothing left to do but to help them discover that this human love is the sign of Christ's love for his Church, they are mistaken. Indeed, very often young people influenced by secularism no longer know at all what conjugal life is. For them, human love is disconnected from ideas of commitment, fidelity, and even more so from indissolubility and fertility. In short, they are ignorant of true human love.

In order for the natural reality of love to open the hearts of the engaged couple to faith, hope, and charity, a *sanatio*, a healing of their view and their practice of human love is necessary. In this sense, preparation for marriage perfectly illustrates the anthropology of *Gaudium et spes*.[2] The Church must teach the young people to discover, admire, and respect their own human nature. As Paul VI used to say, "The path of God leads through man. The discovery of God proceeds by way of the discovery of man."

Engaged couples have to discover the truth of conjugal life: "the intimate partnership of married life and love ... established by the Creator and qualified by His laws".[3] Marriage preparation is therefore first and foremost a school of conjugal life. It is the discovery of the fact that true love between spouses, "a mutual gift of two persons [and an] intimate

---

[2] See GS 14.
[3] GS 48.

union, ... impose total fidelity on the spouses and argue for an unbreakable oneness between them."[4] Here the Church must become the servant and the restorer of the nature of man and woman, because "by their very nature, the institution of matrimony itself and conjugal love are ordained for the procreation and education of children.... Thus a man and a woman ... render mutual help and service to each other through an intimate union of their persons and of their actions."[5]

Marriage preparation must therefore proceed by way of a rediscovery of the beauty and the meaning of the difference between the sexes and of their complementarity, which leads to a true love. Only this "authentic married love is caught up into divine love and is governed and enriched by Christ's redeeming power and the saving activity of the Church."[6] This last point is of capital importance: only an authentic love can become the "matter" for the sacrament of marriage. The counterfeits of human love (a trial arrangement, a union that is not open to new life, homosexual unions) are objectively disordered; they cannot enter into God's plan. It is a matter of the consistency of the divine plan for humanity. God the Savior is not a stranger to God the Creator! The sacramental order is a consecration of the authentic, right natural order. "This love God has judged worthy of special gifts, healing, perfecting, and exalting gifts of grace and of charity."[7] It is therefore extremely important that all who prepare engaged couples for marriage not be content to prepare them for the sacrament. They must set up a school of true human love, a school of authentic conjugal life.

Proclaiming Christ

However, every action of the Church is part of evangelization. We must not be afraid to declare loudly and clearly that the purpose of this school of human love is to proclaim the Good News.

To bring right and true order into one's human life is to perform the work of conversion; it is already to be open to grace. As they learn to experience the natural realities of human love—fidelity, conjugal charity, conjugal friendship, mutual forgiveness, mutual support, openness to new life—the future spouses, therefore, open their hearts to Christ.

[4] Ibid.
[5] Ibid.
[6] GS 48.
[7] GS 49.

In fact, the young engaged couple often discover that they are still far from an authentic love. The school of true conjugal love will be in the first place a school of deliberate choice and, therefore, of renunciation. In order to be willing to make the gift of self, one must be able to renounce selfishness so as to be open to the other; it is necessary to learn to listen, to accept sexual otherness; it is necessary to understand the profound identity of man and of woman. In order to be open to new life, it is necessary to abandon a hedonistic, possessive view of sexuality.[8] True human love is a school of giving, and, consequently, it presupposes an effort and sometimes leads to failures.

A marriage preparation program accompanies the future spouses on this journey, during which they discover that, in order to love in truth, they need help that surpasses human strength. They come to appreciate the necessity of prayer and grace. Even if their faith is wavering or merely incipient, the engaged couple learn that the adventure of natural love, in order to be lived to the end, requires a grace of fortitude. "Christian spouses have a special sacrament by which they are fortified."[9] Here marriage preparation must become instruction in the faith.

But this is only an initial approach. The sacrament of matrimony is indeed much more than a simple aid to human love; it is a true "consecration".[10] Here it is necessary to count on the work of the Holy Spirit in the heart of the just person. Some engaged couples who are filled with wonder by the truth about conjugal love will want to know the source of the Church's teaching. As Pope Francis said forcefully to future spouses: "If you allow yourselves to discover the rich teachings of the Church on love, you will discover that Christianity does not consist of a series of prohibitions which stifle our desire for happiness, but rather a project for life capable of captivating our hearts."[11]

The explicit proclamation of Christ, who gave his life out of love, is necessary for those who want to give themselves in love for life. Marriage preparation includes here a concern for evangelization. Very often one is dealing with couples who do not even know the most basic teachings of the faith. It will be necessary then to set forth the benevolent, merciful plan of God, of which human love is the image and the sacrament of

[8] Cf. GS 47.
[9] GS 48.
[10] Ibid.
[11] Message of Pope Francis for World Youth Day 2015, no. 2.

marriage—the instrument. "For as God of old made Himself present to His people through a covenant of love and fidelity, so now the Savior of men and the Spouse of the Church comes into the lives of married Christians through the sacrament of matrimony."[12]

Marriage preparation thus is a place conducive to the proclamation of the kerygma. The redemptive Incarnation, the manifestation of God's nuptial love for mankind; the sacrifice of the Cross, the place where this love was consummated; the sacramental order, which brings into play the senses and bodies of men in the service of God's plan of love and salvation—all these realities touch the hearts of the engaged couple.

Moreover, the future spouses see that the sacramental efficacy is of immediate concern to them if we explain to them that "the Christian family, which springs from marriage as a reflection of the loving covenant uniting Christ with the Church, and as a participation in that covenant, will manifest to all men Christ's living presence in the world."[13] The human experience of true love is therefore authentic instruction in the Christian faith and a path of conversion.

We have to be clear, however: without the desire for the sacrament, understood as the Church intends it, the celebration of marriage runs the risk of becoming a merely human ceremony. It would be a sort of rite of passage that would have nothing to do with the faith. "When in spite of all efforts, engaged couples show that they reject explicitly and formally what the Church intends to do when the marriage of baptized persons is celebrated, the pastor of souls cannot admit them to the celebration of marriage."[14] Authentic preparation for marriage must therefore go through all the steps: the healing of human love, conversion to authentic conjugal love, openness to prayer and to God's grace, the intention to receive a sacrament that will be a true means of salvation and sanctity. It must strive to obtain the best possible dispositions in the future spouses and not be content with the minimum required for validity.

A conjugal catechumenate

This development cannot be purely intellectual. It is a sort of "catechumenate". This assumes that marriage preparation is not reduced to a series of magisterial teachings. Each engaged person must be able

---

[12] GS 48.
[13] GS 48.
[14] John Paul II, apostolic exhortation *Familiaris consortio* (November 22, 1981) (*FC*), 68.

to meet several times with a priest. Similarly, the priest in charge must be able to observe the journey that has been made in all areas. Here there is a dimension of discernment that is absolutely necessary, in the natural order as well as in the spiritual order. The priest in charge must be able to testify that each of the engaged couples is mature and ready for married life, that each one has asked himself about the concrete possibility of a faithful, indissoluble union, in love and open to new life, with this specific spouse, and not just in general. Likewise, the priest must be able to explain the consistent practice of the Catholic faith, which includes the sacrament of reconciliation, weekly attendance at Sunday Mass, and daily prayer. Of course marriage preparation is not a sort of "bureau of investigation" that determines whether or not the couples are practicing Catholics. Yet, "woe to me if I do not preach the gospel!" (1 Cor 9:16). A program that did not propose a true path of conversion, a true life of holiness in imitation of Christ, would be woeful preparation for marriage.

Let us not forget that the sacraments are made for holiness. By the grace of marriage, spouses are "penetrated with the spirit of Christ, which suffuses their whole lives with faith, hope, and charity. Thus they increasingly advance the perfection of their own personalities, as well as their mutual sanctification."[15] During marriage preparation, therefore, it will be necessary to teach clearly the vocation of everyone to holiness. It would be absurd for priests to hide from baptized persons the dynamism within them under the pretext of taking a pastoral approach. By its very nature, the grace of baptism tends toward holiness. Every baptized person bears this call within him. To allow baptized couples to ignore this call to bear witness by a holy life would in fact be to show profound contempt for them, to refuse to offer them the most precious treasure of the Church. How could anyone propose to them a sort of second-class Christianity by not presenting to them all the demands of sacramental marriage?

That would be a lie and a form of discrimination. It is therefore appropriate to teach everyone that "[t]he constant fulfillment of the duties of this Christian vocation demands notable virtue. For this reason, strengthened by grace for holiness of life, the couple will painstakingly cultivate and pray for steadiness of love, large heartedness, and the spirit of sacrifice."[16]

[15] GS 48.
[16] GS 49.

In marriage, two realities call for one another, as the divine economy itself testifies: the natural institution of marriage and its sacramental dignity. Christian spouses must live these two realities of their conjugal life inseparably. Respect for the natural order of marriage disposes them to enjoy the fruit of the sacrament, and the sacramental order heals, perfects, and elevates their human love.

To prepare for marriage is to play on these two keyboards inseparably, not in a merely doctrinal, didactic way, but by way of heightened awareness, profound assimilation, and evangelization. To be able to define love is one thing; it is another thing entirely to be able to arrange one's life so as to allow for the right expression of love, as an engaged couple or as spouses.

For the sake of convenience, we first suggest a list of points, grouped according to major themes, to be included in a marriage preparation program. Then we will spell out what the sacramental order specifically contributes toward living these realities of marital and family life. But we must not forget that there is reciprocity between the natural order and the sacramental order. Prayer and the sacraments of Eucharist and reconciliation are already a necessary aid in experiencing this preparation for marriage as outlined in the following points.

THE MAJOR THEMES OF MARITAL LIFE

Freedom and self-giving forever

Everyone knows that the freedom of the two future spouses is a prerequisite for the validity of the marriage that they contract.[17] But what is freedom? This notion has suffered too many travesties to be clear to our contemporaries. One fundamental element should be brought out: a free act is a choice. Everything is still possible for someone who does not choose. But as long as he does not choose, nothing is real. Realism lies in choice. Far from being constrictive, choice is the only option that opens us to what is real in life and, thus, to the flourishing of joy. Several consequences follow from this. First, a choice is a sacrifice. Within the context of marriage, this is expressed by the quip: "A man who chooses one woman gives up all the others." That is true. It should be added,

---

[17] *Catechism of the Catholic Church*, no. 1628 (*CCC*).

though, that by not getting engaged, he gives up even more: all the others plus one, since he will not be the husband (in the full sense of the word) of any of them. Incidentally, we often hear it said, too, that such a choice is very imprudent, inasmuch as no one knows the future and no one can really tell whether it will "work". To this objection there are two interconnected answers. First, the choice is prepared. It is an act of the will enlightened by the intellect. To contemplate marrying without preparing for marriage is an inconsiderate, inconsistent act. Secondly, in the sacrament of matrimony, Christ is the principal actor; he who knows the past, the present, and the future takes his part in the sacred bond of the spouses. Christ's presence at the heart of their love strengthens and confirms their commitment.[18]

In order to help the engaged couple to live in freedom even before their marriage, one can recommend to them the experiment of acting more by choice in their daily life. Not only "I must" or "I should", but "I will". And as for their love, one can encourage them to renew in their hearts this choice to love the other on a daily basis. For in marriage, too, their initial commitment will have to be renewed daily. Their "yes" on their wedding day will be their "yes" of every day. All commitment draws its strength from repeated practice.

The difference between the sexes

Marriage preparation should be the place for the peaceful acceptance of the difference and complementarity between man and woman. The Western world wants to deny this difference. *Gender theory* tries to reduce it to a social construct imposed from outside that supposedly mars the freedom of individuals. An authentic human love, in contrast, arrives at a twofold acceptance. Indeed, it is important to accept, first, one's own sexual identity. I receive myself with a sexed body from the hands of the Creator. This identity orients my freedom; it gives it a direction. It is a call to be fully myself as a father (in the case of a man) or as a mother (in the case of a woman). This free and peaceful acceptance of self is the prerequisite for accepting the other in his or her sexual identity. Indeed, the future spouse is perceived and accepted as being different, with his or her own needs, and a different way of understanding and reacting.

[18] Cf. *CCC* 1648.

"Created by Love, that is, endowed in their being with masculinity and femininity,... the human body, with its sex,... contains from the beginning the spousal attribute, that is, the power to express love: precisely that love in which the human person becomes a gift and ... fulfills the very meaning of his being and existence."[19] The acceptance of this otherness opens the doors to an understanding of complementarity. Hence man and woman admire each other; they discover that they need one another. African philosophy says: "Man is nothing without woman, woman is nothing without man, and both are nothing without a third element, which is the child."

It is evident here that the acceptance of our own nature opens us to the Trinity. Man is a being-in-relation. If he loses this orientation, he is imprisoned in his solitude. The experience of the complementarity between man and woman, with all the listening and mutual acceptance that this entails, opens the engaged couple to a life of charity in the light of Trinitarian love.

From celibacy to marriage

The union of a married couple demands first of all that each one be able to leave his single life, the better to choose each other. In this regard we can suggest to the engaged couple an examination of conscience as to what they think about their present management of their priorities, or, we should say, about the order of their charity. "He [God] set in order charity in me."[20] This order of charity is modified in fact by marriage, in which the spouse becomes that first neighbor with whom one is united and to whom fraternal love is shown. "But on the part of the union, the wife ought to be loved more, because she is united with her husband, as one flesh, according to Matthew 19:6: 'Therefore now they are not two, but one flesh.'"[21]

The union of a couple requires above all that each party detach himself from his own family. What else does the saying in Genesis mean: "Therefore a man leaves his father and his mother [as a woman does

---

[19] John Paul II, General Audience, January 16, 1980; English translation from *Man and Woman He Created Them: A Theology of the Body*, trans. Michael Waldstein (Boston: Pauline Books & Media, 2006), 185–90, citation at 185–86.

[20] Canticle of Canticles [Song of Solomon] 2:4, Douay-Rheims.

[21] Saint Thomas, *Summa Theologiae* II-II, q. 26, a. 11.

too]"?[22] Here two important, connected ideas are to be ingrained in the everyday life of those who are preparing to marry.

A child who marries leaves the cell into which he was born to found a new cell, the nucleus of which will have the firmness of the conjugal love that he will share with his spouse. Many sufferings of young married couples result from a misunderstanding, on their part or on that of their parents, of the new place that their families of origin occupy in the building of their new familial cell. Many instances of paternal or maternal intrusion into their new home will help the newlyweds to become aware of their proper autonomy.

Yet at the same time they must take into account another reality that must be harmonized with the first. It is good and unavoidable[23] to love one's parents, with that coloring of love which is respect for them. Leaving one's father and mother cannot mean that one stops loving them. "A man does not in all respects leave his father and mother for the sake of his wife: for in certain cases a man ought to succor his parents rather than his wife. He does, however, leave all his kinfolk and cleaves to his wife as regards the union of carnal connection and co-habitation."[24]

Thus the unique human heart of each member of the engaged couple is, so to speak, crisscrossed by these two loves: love for his future spouse and love for his parents. It is not uncommon for there to be adverse incidents in the story of an engaged couple that have torn them apart. To become aware of these two necessary and beneficial loves and to learn to harmonize them correctly is a true path of conversion. The engaged couple then understand, from personal experience, how the growth of these two loves, each in its proper place, is mutually beneficial and strengthens the human heart.

To know oneself in truth

Loving someone else requires loving oneself. The act of charity that we learn in the catechism puts it well: "O my God, I love you above all things because you are all-good and worthy of all my love, and I love my neighbor as myself for love of you."[25] Now, in order to love oneself, it

---

[22] Gen 2:24.

[23] We mean that no one is indifferent toward his parents. The resentment that some people feel toward them is proportionate to the expectation of wounded love.

[24] Saint Thomas, *Summa Theologiae* II-II, q. 26, a. 11 ad 1.

[25] An "Act of Love" with slightly different wording is among the prayers in Appendix A of the *Compendium of the Catechism of the Catholic Church*.

is good to learn gradually who one is, so as not to demand of the other what is our own responsibility. Indeed, we have a very deep-seated tendency to seek in a relationship with someone else things that might make up for our own shortcomings, especially for things that we lacked in our childhood. It would be absolutely unfair to demand that someone else be our crutch. The spouse's love can help us to face childhood traumas, yes. But no, we cannot expect the spouse to heal them. To know oneself is to agree to take oneself in hand in an adult way so as to offer to the other a person who respects himself and, to paraphrase a verse from a psalm, "who holds his life in his hand continually".[26]

How can we help engaged couples to make progress in their self-knowledge? Marriage preparation is not a venture in personal development. It is, however, a good opportunity to help engaged couples to express their different views of things, of events, of persons, and to make them perhaps discover for themselves the distorting prisms through which they tend to regard them. This is much easier, incidentally, inasmuch as young people today find it easier to speak to one another simply and sincerely. This is no doubt one of their finest gifts.

Listening to one another

Communication is at the service of communion. To say that is to emphasize its importance in the context of preparation for marriage, which is defined as "a whole manner and communion of life".[27] People today generally insist a lot on communication. It has become a profession, no doubt because never before have people communicated so badly. It seems paradoxical to stress this shortcoming at a time when the means of communication are more numerous and effective than in any other period of history. However, this is only apparently a paradox. It is not enough to have good tools available; it is necessary also to know how to use them. In this regard, education and the acquisition of virtues are necessary in order to fight against intemperance in the use of the means of social communication, with their immediacy and prolixity, and to develop a constructive communication of love. Now young couples encounter all sorts of difficulties in their communication, which may wrongly lead them to doubt their love and the relevance of their engagement. In fact, it is necessary to teach them to measure the means

[26] Ps 119:109.
[27] GS 50.

of communication by its object. One does not transmit the same information by text message and by telephone, by a letter or in a face-to-face meeting. Helping them along this path is part of the engagement period, which appears to be a true "catechumenate of love".

More profoundly, Western societies have a very restrictive practice of listening, a form of listening that one could describe as cerebral or analytical. And that is not the prerogative of men! We are reminded here of Saint-Exupéry and his Little Prince: "Here is my secret. It is very simple. Only with the heart can one see rightly." This listening with the heart is particularly decisive in cultivating love. "The union of hearts! The nuances that differentiate the love of the man and that of the woman are innumerable. Neither of the partners can expect to be loved exactly as he loves. A very unifying practice is to share the joys and, even more so, the sufferings of one's heart."[28] To listen with the heart is to welcome, to receive the other without judging, without analyzing, because he is the other and he is a highly respectable person. Someone who practices this art or this virtue knows how to love, and he discovers that language has only a utilitarian function, whereas to listen to a person confide or express pain or a feeling is to receive a gift. And listening is sometimes the only love we can give to someone who is in pain. To love is to listen, to receive the other as he is and not as I would like him to be. It is easy to make a transition here and to speak about prayer as an expression of love. To be able to listen to God, to welcome him in our heart: Is that not to love?

Professional life, domestic life, and personal life

A recurring difficulty in married life has to do with what we might call balance in life. Three aspects of life seem to compete with each other: family life (which includes marital life), professional life, and personal life. To choose the married state is to reflect, even during the engagement, on how to harmonize these three dimensions.

The man and the woman, who are dependent on the society in which they were born and have lived, owe to it everything they have received from it (religion, language, culture, history ...). In founding a family, the basic cell of society, they share in perpetuating that society and, so

---

[28] John Paul II, Homily in Kinshasa, May 3, 1980. (Translated from French.)

to speak, strive to pay their debt of gratitude. Likewise, when they share in the transmission of what they have received and in the development of society by some professional activity (in the broad sense of activity ordered to the good of society, so that it includes volunteer work also). "The interpersonal relations within the sanctuary of the family must overflow outside of it; otherwise the Christian home would run the risk of being a refuge, an ivory tower."[29] Yet the human person's sole purpose is not the common good of society. He is ultimately ordered to God. He does not derive all his value and dignity from the fact that he is ordered to the common good. This is what Saint John XXIII meant when he declared that society is for man and not man for society. And in this way these three components of human activity—social, familial, and personal—fall into their proper place.

The balance among these three aspects is delicate. It is easily disrupted, for example, by neglecting one's personal life (rest, prayer, reading, music ...), which is characterized by a certain gratuitousness. Thus John Paul II recalled that "each of the spouses must reserve for himself some moments of solitude with God, a heart-to-heart conversation in which the spouse is not the primary concern. This indispensable personal life with God does not prevent spouses from having all their familial and marital life in common—far from it."[30] One could also invest so much of oneself in professional life that the family would suffer as a result. In short, it is appropriate to ask oneself the question about harmonizing these three components, while discerning the excesses to which one's temperament or habits expose the future couple.

On the same subject, another difficulty arises with regard to working women. This subject cannot be ignored. For financial reasons or for the sake of her personal equilibrium, the woman may choose to work. It is absolutely necessary, then, that she become aware of the sacrifice that her absence from her children might be for her and that she choose to make it deliberately so that it is not a source of anxiety and sadness for her. Although some professional activities are incompatible with the necessary presence of a mother in the home, other activities fit perfectly well into that setting. We might add that the presence of an unhappy

---

[29]John Paul II, Address to Catholic Family Associations, November 10, 1980. (Translated from French.)

[30]John Paul II, Homily in Kinshasa, May 3, 1980. (Translated from French.)

mother at home with her children no doubt does not offer them what they will need for balanced growth. Facing the truth in this matter, too, is a fine school for conversion during the engagement.

Body and fertility

The area where Western societies no doubt have the greatest need of being evangelized is the area of the body and sexuality. The latter is no longer viewed as a reality integrated into the human person; it is as though detached, autonomous. The carnal act is no longer the encounter of two persons; it is at the service of a psychological, physical, chemical reaction. As for the unborn child, he is often regarded as a threat, to the point where it is necessary to protect oneself from him and to wage against him the most merciless chemical warfare. Carnal relations, turned in on themselves, are no longer the expression of love, but that of narcissism for two.

The first point to emphasize in the context of marriage preparation is precisely the place of carnal relations in love. They are the expression of the total, irrevocable gift of self that the spouses make to one another. That means that this gift must be total, which for baptized persons includes the definitive, public commitment that is at the heart of the sacrament of matrimony. From this perspective, carnal relations before marriage would be a lie and a form of cheating. It is important to recall this so as to situate the love of the engaged couple within "the splendor of the truth". It is necessary to go farther in order to be truly consistent. With regard to the physical expression of their love, the engaged couple will have to discern the legitimate gestures that cause their love to grow and to abstain from those that are not in keeping with their state in life. Indeed, some gestures are objectively preliminaries to the conjugal act, for which the engaged couple are not ready. Furthermore, a certain sort of physical intimacy may prove to be inappropriate and trouble the serenity of their love. In this area, marriage preparation is a period of asceticism and mutual respect[31] that promotes the clarity of love and freedom in making the future choice. It is conducive to an authentic evangelization of the body and of the sexual instinct.

---

[31] "Those who are *engaged to marry* are called to live chastity in continence. They should see in this time of testing a discovery of mutual respect, an apprenticeship in fidelity, and the hope of receiving one another from God. They should reserve for marriage the expressions of affection that belong to married love. They will help each other grow in chastity" (*CCC* 2350).

John Paul II forcefully challenged young people: "Do not be deceived by the empty words of those who ridicule chastity or your capacity for self-control. The strength of your future married love depends on the strength of your present commitment to learning true love, a chastity which includes refraining from all sexual relations outside of marriage."[32] This requirement must be presented by those who prepare couples for marriage. It is a lofty form of respect for the human person. To conceal it would be to disdain and infantilize those whom one judges *a priori* to be incapable of experiencing true love. As Paul VI said: "Now it is an outstanding manifestation of charity toward souls to omit nothing from the saving doctrine of Christ; but this must always be joined with tolerance and charity, as Christ Himself showed in His conversations and dealings with men. For when He came, not to judge, but to save the world, was He not bitterly severe toward sin, but patient and abounding in mercy toward sinners?"[33] This mercy should be made clear to those who are preparing for marriage, and it should also be practiced by them and between them. Thus one can encourage recourse to the sacrament of reconciliation and the Eucharist, in which they will renew their intention to keep their love pure and from which they will draw Christ's own strength.

The time of marriage preparation will also be a time to reeducate the couple and reform their concept of the carnal act, which has been distorted by the milieu of a hedonistic society that regards pleasure as the purpose of bodily union. Pleasure is, rather, the fruit of the union of two persons, body and soul, in love. Besides, it would be better to speak about "joy", which is more inclusive of the spiritual and emotional aspects of persons, without omitting the specifically corporeal dimension. "The union of the spouses' bodies is willed by God himself as the expression of the even deeper union of their minds and hearts. Performed with respect as well as tenderness, it renews the dynamism and the vigor of their solemn commitment, of their first 'yes'."[34]

The future spouses will thus have to rediscover an esteem for the beauty of sexuality according to God's plan. "Sexual actions are 'words' that reveal our hearts. *The Lord wants us to use our sexuality according to his plan.* He expects us to 'speak' truthfully."[35]

[32]John Paul II, Meeting with the Youth of Uganda, February 6, 1993.

[33]Paul VI, encyclical *Humanae vitae* (July 25, 1968) (*HV*), 29.

[34]John Paul II, Homily in Kinshasa, May 3, 1980. (Translated from French.)

[35]John Paul II, Meeting with the Youth of Uganda, February 6, 1993.

While explaining the beauty and dignity of the union of bodies in marriage, as well as the legitimacy of the physical joy given to the other, it is judicious to recall that this joy may involve patient adjustments; the ideal images presented nowadays of these adjustments sometimes misrepresent the humility of our corporeal condition. Mutual physical joy will be more readily achieved the more it takes into account all the dimensions of the person and when it is the result of a truly human act and not of an anarchical, wild instinct masked as spontaneity or ignoring the limitations of human nature. Finally, knowledge about natural methods of regulating fertility will help the engaged couple to restore "the inseparable connection, established by God, which man on his own initiative may not break, between the unitive significance and the procreative significance which are both inherent to the marriage act."[36]

THE SACRAMENTAL ORDER

To experience the faith

All the realities that we have just mentioned, however, are not the heart of marriage as a sacrament. They are not the essential thing, and yet it is absolutely necessary that they be put in place. Let us explain this in the words of Benedict XVI:

> We must have clearly in mind what the essential is that we want and must transmit to others, and what are the *preambula* in situations in which we can take the first steps. Of course, a certain preliminary ethical education is a basic step even today. This is also what ancient Christianity did. Cyprian, for example, tells us that first his life was totally dissolute; then, living in the catechumenal community, he learned a fundamental ethic and thus, the way to God unfolded before him. And at the Easter Vigil Saint Ambrose said: So far we have spoken of morals, now we come to the mysteries. They had made the journey of the *preambula fidei* with a fundamental ethical education that created the readiness to understand God's mystery.[37]

Setting up an authentic human love and giving up the corrupt imitations of this love is therefore a first step, a *preambulum*. "But the question

[36] HV 12.
[37] Benedict XVI, Address to the Clergy of the Diocese of Rome, February 7, 2008.

must always be: what is the essential? What must be discovered? What do I want to give? And here I continue to repeat: the essential is God. If we do not speak of God, if God is not discovered, we always remain with secondary things."[38] Therefore, once the natural first steps are in place, it is absolutely necessary to situate human love within God's plan of salvation.

Now those active in marriage preparation run up against a difficulty here. As Pope Francis emphasized very recently, many young people prefer cohabitation "with limited responsibility"[39] to marriage because they are afraid of failure. The many, many divorces that they observe in their families prevent them from thinking that authentic married life is possible in the long term. Even though deep down they desire an indissoluble union, in fact they cannot manage to believe that it is possible. This is a crisis of trust and faith in God and consequently a crisis of confidence in human love and in the human ability to be faithful. John Paul II did not hesitate to blame this fear on "the short-winded culture typical of the wealthy nations"[40] characterized by alienation from God.

How can this crisis of faith and confidence be overcome? We would like to point out two remedies. First, it is necessary to show young people, or rather to make them experience the fact, that Christian married life is possible. Indeed, very often engaged couples are like Saint Cyprian, who exclaimed: "In seeing Christians I thought: it is an impossible life, this cannot be done in our world! Then, however, meeting some of them, joining their company and letting myself be guided in the catechumenate, in this process of conversion to God, I gradually understood: it is possible!"[41]

Therefore, it appears to be of capital importance that future spouses be able to benefit from the witness of Christian couples. The latter can testify to their joys, the difficulties they have overcome; in short, they can show that Christian married life is possible. But it is necessary to go farther. The engaged couple must experience Christian life as a life of holiness. Marriage preparation should therefore include the experience of life with a parish community that is fervent and consistent in its faith. How can anyone desire to lead a Christian life if he does not see it achieved

[38] Ibid.

[39] Pope Francis, General Audience, April 29, 2015.

[40] John Paul II, To the Young People of Turin, September 3, 1988.

[41] Benedict XVI, Address to the Clergy of the Diocese of Rome, February 22, 2007.

concretely anywhere? In this sense, spiritual centers and religious houses can be "oases" where one can experience Christian life in action.

> Thus, the first point is experience, which also opens the door to knowledge. In this regard, the "catechumenate" lived in a new way—that is, as a common journey through life, a common experience of the possibility of living in this way—is of paramount importance.
>
> Only if there is a certain experience can one also understand. I remember a piece of advice that Pascal gave to a non-believer friend. He told him: "Try to do what a believer does, then you will see from this experience that it is all logical and true."[42]

Marriage preparation should offer this experience to future spouses. Only then will they be able to understand that "the indissolubility of marriage finds its ultimate truth in the plan that God has manifested in His revelation: He wills and He communicates the indissolubility of marriage as a fruit, a sign, and a requirement of the absolutely faithful love that God has for man and that the Lord Jesus has for the Church."[43]

Putting the Cross back at the center

The second remedy that we want to recommend to cure the engaged couple's lack of faith and confidence is something for which priests are directly responsible. We are afraid to preach the Cross, we are afraid to preach Jesus crucified, we are afraid of suffering! Yes, the life of every married couple has its difficulties, its crises. Often the time comes in married life when the difference of the other spouse becomes an unbearable burden. Then comes the temptation to separate. "Precisely in crises, in bearing the moment in which it seems that no more can be borne, new doors and a new beauty of love truly open.... Even a grape, in order to ripen, does not only need the sun but also the rain, not only the day but also the night.... I believe that the fact the Lord bears the stigmata for eternity has a symbolic value."[44]

We cannot do without the Cross. It is the prerequisite for an authentic Christian life. We must have the courage to preach its beauty to young

---

[42] Ibid.
[43] FC 20.
[44] Benedict XVI, Meeting with the Priests of the Diocese of Albano, August 3, 2006.

engaged couples. The physical experience of the Cross is a grace that is absolutely necessary for our growth in the Christian faith and a providential opportunity to be conformed to Christ so as to enter into the depths of the ineffable. In piercing the Heart of Jesus, the soldier's lance opened up a great mystery, for it went farther than the Heart of Christ; it opened up God; it went, so to speak, into the middle of the Trinity. The Cross, suffering, a crisis experienced in union with Christ is a dimension of Christian marriage. Calvary is the vantage point from which we can see everything with the eyes of Christ and therefore understand what true love is. And so, as John Paul II recalled, "Spouses are therefore the permanent reminder to the Church of what happened on the Cross."[45]

The *Catechism* puts it forcefully: "It is by following Christ, renouncing themselves, and taking up their crosses that spouses will be able to 'receive' the original meaning of marriage and live it with the help of Christ. This grace of Christian marriage is a fruit of Christ's cross."[46]

Of course, this preaching must be accompanied by the reminder that Jesus has not loaded spouses down with a burden that is too heavy and impossible to carry. He came to reestablish the original order that had been disrupted by sin, and, in coming to restore the indissolubility of marriage, "he himself gives the strength and grace to live marriage in the new dimension of the Reign of God."[47]

It is therefore necessary to present marriage to engaged couples as a spiritual journey in which the spouses follow Christ in his Paschal Mystery. John Paul II was not afraid to insist:

> The loving relationship participates in the growth of the spouse. It is a service rendered to the other, following the example of Christ the servant who washed the feet of his disciples on the evening of Holy Thursday. Marital life is never free of trials, which cause the couple to go through painful moments in which love and trust in the other and in oneself seem to waver. The spouses will derive strength by uniting themselves to the sentiments of Christ during the night before Good Friday. Many have experienced this: going through a trial together can help purify their love. But there are also moments of intense joy resulting from their communion in love. These moments recall that, beyond all suffering, there is

[45] FC 13.
[46] CCC 1615.
[47] Ibid.

the brilliant light and the definitive victory of Easter morning. Thus the sacrament of marriage has a Paschal structure.[48]

Thus the sacramental order is situated within the whole life of grace in which God has already made the couple sharers by their baptism.[49] This is why it is appropriate for the couple to regard their engagement as a time for prayer and receiving the sacraments for the purpose of increasing their love as well as a time of catechesis on the nature of the sacrament that they are preparing to administer to each other.

Prayer and the sacraments

In light of this spirit of faith, marriage preparation must insist on the need for the future spouses to pray together. A Christian married couple is a living cell of the Church, an *ecclesiola*, or "little church". The life of that cell is its prayer. If the engaged couple do not acquire the habit of praying for one another and even together, how would they pray as spouses?

"Wherever people pray together the Lord makes himself present with that power which can also dissolve 'sclerosis' of the heart, that hardness of heart which, according to the Lord, is the real reason for divorce. Nothing else, only the Lord's presence, helps us to truly relive what the Creator wanted at the outset and which the Redeemer renewed."[50]

Marriage preparation must therefore take it upon itself to be a school of prayer, and specifically of prayer as a couple. Praying as a pair, praying in the family, is something that can be learned. Benedict XVI taught: "In your prayer together, ask the Lord to watch over and increase your love and to purify it of all selfishness."[51]

Every human life is also marred by sin. The relationship of love and charity between the engaged couple, then the spouses, is wounded every day by multiple imperfections: failures to listen, irritations, flaring tempers, disappointments. The couple will have to discover the value of forgiveness that is asked for, given, and received daily. Marriage preparation

[48]John Paul II, Meeting with Families, Saint Anne d'Auray, September 20, 1996. (Translated from French.)
[49]We cannot address here the case of a non-baptized fiancé(e), although the subject is increasingly timely.
[50]Benedict XVI, Address to the Clergy of the Diocese of Rome, March 2, 2006.
[51]Benedict XVI, Message for World Youth Day, April 1, 2007.

is a propitious time to rediscover what true forgiveness is, not the denial of the sin, but recognition of the value of the person, above and beyond his guilt. "What sort of love would it be that stopped short of forgiveness? This highest form of union involves the whole being who, deliberately and lovingly, agrees not to dwell on the offense and instead to believe that a future is still possible. Forgiveness is an eminent form of gift, which affirms the other's dignity in recognizing him for who he is, beyond what he does. Everyone who forgives enables the one who is forgiven to discover the infinite grandeur of God's forgiveness."[52] And so it is only right that receiving forgiveness presupposes acknowledging one's sin and repenting. Future spouses will learn to do this quite simply; they will discover firsthand that forgiveness draws them closer together, that their love will be strengthened by it. This experience will make them more receptive to the divine mercy. They will be able to return to the practice of regular reception of the sacrament of reconciliation.

A house in which the words "I'm sorry" are never uttered begins to lack air, and the flood waters begin to choke those who live inside. So many wounds, so many scrapes and bruises are the result of a lack of these precious words: "I am sorry." Marital life is so often torn apart by fights ... the "plates will even start flying", but let me give you a word of advice: never finish the day without making peace with one another. Listen to me carefully: did you fight with your wife or husband? Kids—did you fight with your parents? Did you seriously argue? That's not a good thing, but it's not really that which is the problem: the problem arises only if this feeling hangs over into the next day. So if you've fought, do not let the day end without making peace with your family.[53]

Likewise, future spouses will have to learn to thank each other regularly for their love, which is not something owed but a favor, a gift, a present. This "thank you" of the engaged couple is a true education in giving thanks. It will give the couple a renewed sense of the Eucharist. In this sense, marriage preparation should include common times of Eucharistic adoration in which the future spouses can discover that the most intimate of the goods they have in common is Christ. Jesus in

---

[52] John Paul II, Meeting with Families, Saint Anne d'Auray, September 20, 1996. (Translated from French.)

[53] Pope Francis, General Audience, May 13, 2015.

the Eucharist, adored, loved, and prayed to together, unites the couple much more profoundly than any human reality.

> "May I?", "thank you", and "pardon me". Indeed, these expressions open up the way to living well in your family, to living in peace. They are simple expressions, but not so simple to put into practice! They hold much power: the power to keep home life intact even when tested with a thousand problems. But if they are absent, little holes can start to crack open and the whole thing may even collapse.... We must become firmly determined to educate others to be grateful and appreciative.... Gratitude ... stands at the very core of the faith of the believer. A Christian who does not know how to thank has lost the very "language" of God.[54]

Marriage, path to holiness

Finally, marriage preparation can become a true catechesis on the sacramental order. The engaged couple know that their intimate love needs gestures and signs in order to become effective. This experience will make them more receptive to the need for the sacraments: sensible, efficacious signs of grace.

Their personal experience will open their minds to the logic of the love of the Incarnation. They will learn from experience that, just as their entire personal life must be consistent with their mutual love, so, too, their whole life must be unified in the light of God. It must be explained to them, therefore, that the sacrament can be fruitful only if their lives are well disposed to receive it. Marriage preparation presupposes in this regard an examination of conscience. The future spouses must ask themselves: Is there anything in my life opposed to the fullness of marital love? Is there anything in my life opposed to the fullness of God's love?

In this sense marriage is governed by the logic of baptism. Baptism immerses us in the death and Resurrection of Christ, and so "all the faithful of Christ, of whatever rank or status, are called to the fullness of the Christian life and to the perfection of charity."[55] For young baptized persons who are called to experience human married love, the only possible way of holiness is sacramental marriage. It is altogether impossible

---

[54] Ibid.

[55] Second Vatican Council, Dogmatic Constitution on the Church, *Lumen gentium* (November 21, 1964), 40.

to claim, as one sometimes hears, that some are not called to sacramental marriage and that the Church ought to "bless non-sacramentally" more or less temporary unions that are supposedly steps in preparation for marriage. *"Without the bond of marriage, sexual relations are a lie.* And for Christians, marriage means sacramental marriage."[56] It is necessary to be clear: all Christians living a life of marital love are called to conjugal holiness, for which sacramental marriage is the sole means. This is a necessary consequence of the teaching of Vatican II about the universal call to holiness. It would be a very serious mistake to allow couples to think during marriage preparation that some other way was possible. That would be tantamount to offering the couple a form of conjugal life cut off from baptism and grace. For the Church, that would be the same as refusing to offer to everyone the call to the perfection of charity. It would be tantamount to institutionalizing lukewarmness and mediocrity and abandoning the prophetic vocation of every Christian.

Yes, in this sense every Christian is a martyr, a witness to the radical claims of the Gospel. Marriage preparation must proclaim this, too. Authentic Christian life presupposes a break, a choice. "My little children, you are not of the world.... If the world hated me, it will hate you too" (cf. Jn 15:18). In preparing couples for marriage, the Church prepares witnesses—in other words, martyrs—of God's love for mankind. Now this love is faithful and irrevocable.

Marriage is a witness for the whole Church. "The domestic Church must become a visible sign of God for all mankind. In looking at the lives of Christian couples, men today must touch something of God's universal love."[57] We have recently had the grace of seeing several married couples beatified—I am thinking about the parents of the Little Flower or of the Beltrames. I do not want to forget in this regard the splendid example of Shahbaz Misih, aged thirty, and of his wife, Shama Bibi, who was twenty-four, who were both burned alive for their faith in an oven where bricks were being baked, on November 4, 2014, in the province of Punjab, in Pakistan, leaving three children, and while Shama was pregnant. Their witness of faith is the best example to give to those who want to prepare in truth for Christian marriage.

---

[56]John Paul II, Meeting with the Youth of Uganda, February 6, 1993.
[57]John Paul II, Address to Catholic Family Associations, November 10, 1980. (Translated from French.)

The Christian love of spouses has for its example Christ, who gives himself totally to the Church, and it is situated within his Paschal Mystery of death and Resurrection, of loving sacrifice, joy, and hope.... In this mysterious economy of grace, spouses strengthen their affection by fixing their gaze on Christ. This is why, in Christian antiquity, they used to give an account of this dimension of grace by depicting Christ in the midst of spouses.[58]

Preparation for the sacrament of matrimony therefore presupposes a true human and spiritual conversion, a radical change that affects all aspects of life. This conversion is the criterion for the full fruitfulness of the sacrament, which can truly elevate human love and make of it the instrument for the sanctification of the spouses. Then marital love—elevated, transfigured, and consecrated—will give glory to God. Then the human couple will form a true *ecclesiola*, or little church, in which each act of love, which is simultaneously human and divine, will truly give worship to God and will have a missionary fruitfulness.

Benedict XVI summarized it as follows: "Preparation for marriage becomes ever more fundamental and necessary.... We must revive their capacity for listening to nature.... [The preparation] must be a rectification of the voice of nature, of the Creator, within us, a rediscovery, beyond what ['everyone else' is doing], of what our own being intimately tells us.... These preparatory courses for marriage ... must help couples reach the true decision of marriage in accordance with the Creator and the Redeemer."[59] Let us not hesitate, therefore, to borrow from Pope Francis the vigorous, missionary words that he spoke to the young volunteers at World Youth Day in Rio: "Yes, I am asking you to rebel against this culture that sees everything as temporary and that ultimately believes you are incapable of responsibility, that believes you are incapable of true love. I have confidence in you, and I pray for you. Have the courage 'to swim against the tide'. And also have the courage to be happy."[60]

[58]John Paul II, Mass for Families, Panama, May 5, 1983. (Translated from French.)

[59]Benedict XVI, Meeting with the Clergy of the Diocese of Belluno-Feltre and Treviso, July 24, 2007.

[60]Pope Francis to Volunteers at World Youth Day, Rio de Janeiro, July 28, 2013.

Christian Marriage

The Reality and Pastoral Care

Jorge L. Cardinal Urosa Savino

INTRODUCTION

Right on target, as Saint John Paul II was in 1980, Pope Francis has decided that the family should be the theme of his first synod. The Holy Father thus points out the importance of this topic for the world and for the Church in our day.

And naturally, in speaking about the family, it is necessary to speak about marriage, a human institution present in all cultures. Every nation, in its own way, considers it important and not only celebrates it but also surrounds it with legal formalities: prerequisites, enumerated rights and duties of those who contract marriage, public ceremony, and official registers. For us Catholics, marriage is a basic element of the family, since it is the basis and origin thereof, the thing that starts it and sustains it over time, the thing that gives it life and continuity.

The Church not only promotes, praises, and defends marriage, but also celebrates it liturgically. In fact, she considers it one of the seven sacraments, instruments and signs of grace and salvation for the contracting parties and their children, and gives it a legal structure so as to protect the rights and specify the duties of the spouses. Marriage between baptized persons has always been considered the sacred union of a man and a woman, a sign of the union between Christ and the Church. For this very reason it is a perpetual, indissoluble union. Only because of the hardness of heart of the ancient people of Israel, Jesus Christ himself tells us, did Moses allow a man to put away his wife with a certificate

Jorge L. Cardinal Urosa Savino is the archbishop of Caracas, Santiago de Venezuela.

of divorce. But he immediately adds that marriage is actually indissoluble (see Mk 10:1–12).

This synod on the family convoked by Pope Francis is taking place in two sessions: one extraordinary session, which was already celebrated in October 2014, and the other ordinary, which will be held in October of this year [2015]. In the reflections by the bishops in the *Relatio synodi* [synod report] of the extraordinary session in October 2014, considerable space was devoted to the very important theme of marriage. And rightly so, since this institution is fundamental for the family and for the future of the Church, and it has a profoundly religious character as the sacrament of the New Covenant, a unique and solemn form with which Christ communicates his grace to the faithful. Reflecting on this institution, in the light of revealed faith and with the eyes of mercy, is all the more important nowadays inasmuch as innovating trends have emerged, even in ecclesial circles, some of which go against the perennial tradition of the Church and threaten to dissolve and deal a fatal blow to the institution of ecclesiastical marriage.

This essay is devoted to that institution, which is fundamental for the Church and society, and will point out only a few of the more important aspects of marriage and, above all, the necessity of promoting it in pastoral ministry as a fundamental element of the Church. Promoting the very great importance of the conjugal union sanctified by the sacrament of matrimony is key to the life of the Church now and in the ages to come.

THE PRESENT SITUATION OF MARRIAGE AND THE FAMILY

We are no doubt very much aware of the difficult situation that affects marriage in the modern world and of the difficulties with which it has to cope. It is not just now that we are taking these into account. Back in 1965, the Second Vatican Council pointed out several problems that cast a shadow over the family and the institution of marriage (*Gaudium et spes* 47). This situation, which Pope Saint John Paul II also reflected very realistically in his apostolic exhortation *Familiaris consortio*, has been getting worse in our day. Therefore the *Relatio synodi* of the extraordinary session of the synod held in October 2014 points out many features of the predicament of the family and marriage in today's world. Among other things, it is necessary today to add the trend that claims to treat the union between persons of the same sex as if it were a true marriage.

Pope Francis, too, has touched on the difficult situation of the family and marriage in his Wednesday catecheses. The reality is worrisome, because although the Catholic Church and the Christian churches promote marriage as the fundamental basis of the nuclear family, the trends in the modern world are opposed to this institution. Indeed, besides the *de facto* unions in many countries of Latin America and the many marriages that end in divorce, today in urban society in the West there is a constant increase in the number of "trial unions", couples who are united temporarily, without any further commitment.

There is an additional problem that I would like to highlight. The secularizing tendency has made its presence felt in the Church, too, and therefore in some places little time or importance is allotted to what are, strictly speaking, the religious and sacramental aspects of marriage. This explains why in some places the pastoral care of families devotes so little attention to the sacramental, religious, and spiritual aspect of marriage, and as a result the spouses have little awareness of the fact that the celebration of the sacrament is an encounter with and in Christ and little appreciation of the greatness of the institution of marriage and of the new reality that comes into being with their vows and the nuptial blessing. They pay attention to the medical, psychological, or sociological aspects of married life, but little truly religious and spiritual preparation for marriage is offered to engaged Catholics. Adequate preparation is lacking, both in the family and in the parish. The engaged couple enter marriage with a weak religious life and with little awareness of the conditions and the spiritual and moral demands of married life.

Moreover, indirect challenges to the greatness and importance of marriage, such as those implied by the theory that divorced and remarried persons could, under certain conditions, be admitted to sacramental Communion, do nothing at all to help strengthen the institution of marriage or, therefore, the Christian family.

Most certainly, the general awareness of the nature and greatness of Christian marriage has been growing weaker in society and among young Catholics. This is a major challenge for the life and future of the Church that we must confront as Christian families, educators, and pastors.

MARRIAGE: A SUPERNATURAL, TRANSFORMING REALITY

Conscious of the treasures that she possesses, the Church has proclaimed over the centuries the sublime nature of Christian marriage, resulting from its sacramental character, which makes it essentially supernatural and transforms the conjugal union between baptized persons.

Its institution

Christ manifested his power and goodness for the first time during the celebration of the wedding feast at Cana (cf. Jn 2:1–11). The *Catechism of the Catholic Church* tells us that "the Church attaches great importance to Jesus' presence at the wedding at Cana. She sees in it the confirmation of the goodness of marriage and the proclamation that thenceforth marriage will be an efficacious sign of Christ's presence" (*CCC* 1613).

In his Letter to the Ephesians, Saint Paul devotes lovely words to the union of spouses, then describes it as the sign of the sacrificial, loving, and spousal union between Christ and his Church: "Husbands, love your wives, as Christ loved the Church and gave himself up for her ... as Christ [takes care of] the Church.... 'For this reason a man shall leave his father and mother and be joined to his wife, and the two shall become one flesh.' This is a great mystery, and I mean in reference to Christ and the Church" (cf. Eph 5:25–32). Christian marriage is symbolic of the union between Christ and the Church, and this significance, no doubt, leads the Church to consider it a sacrament, in other words, a sign of a supernatural reality that communicates God's life, strength, help, and grace to the spouses so that they might live out their married life and their commitment with complete fidelity and always in love. In order to live up to this ideal, in order to be able to fulfill the greatest commandment of the new law of Christ, which is love (Jn 15:12), the spouses receive the necessary grace in the nuptial sacrament.

Its nature

Because it is one of the seven sacraments, by virtue both of its sacramental nature and also of the fact that it transforms the contracting parties, marriage is an instrument of the spiritual renewal of the spouses so that they might be a new reality. Because it is a sacrament, it converts the spouses into a symbol of the love of Christ for the world. From this sacramental nature also springs grace, strength, and continual help so that they might thoroughly live out their commitment to mutual self-giving in spite of the difficulties and in the midst of the adverse circumstances that life deals to every human being.

Its indissolubility

The Lord left us clear teachings about the unity and indissolubility of marriage, which even surprised some of his disciples (Mt 19:1–9; Mk 10:1–12; Lk 16:18). To claim to debate them, to question them, or to empty them of meaning is to make Jesus' words pointless. It is not taking the Lord seriously. Saint Paul in his Letter to the Romans repeats these teachings (Rom 7:2–3). The Lord's words imply that, as a sign of love between Christ and the Church, the marital contract creates a perpetual and exclusive bond between the spouses, an indissoluble, lifelong bond, and presupposes and demands the unity of the couple, in other words, implies monogamy. Let us listen to the teachings of the *Catechism of the Catholic Church*: "Thus *the marriage bond* has been established by God himself in such a way that a marriage concluded and consummated between baptized persons can never be dissolved. This bond, which results from a free human act of the spouses and their consummation of the marriage, is a reality, henceforth irrevocable, and gives rise to a covenant guaranteed by God's fidelity. The Church does not have the power to contravene this disposition of divine wisdom" (*CCC* 1640).

In fact, the nature of the authentic personal love of the spouses demands permanence, continuity, fidelity, and perseverance in the conjugal communion. In another respect, this indissolubility, with the stability that it entails, is one of the great contributions of marriage to society and to a nation. We mean the basis for the stability and permanence of the family as a stable social union that provides education, common life, human support, and economic production. Indissolubility takes the spouses seriously and is a sign of respect, dedication, and affection; it promotes the constant search for the common good, implies a willingness to forgive, help, and support the spouse in any circumstance whatsoever, in adversity and prosperity, in sickness and in health. Indissolubility is the love that leads the married person to grow old lovingly with his spouse. To question indissolubility is not in keeping with Christ's words, with the teachings of the Church through the centuries, or with Catholic moral teaching about sexuality.

Its necessity

Christian marriage, with its sacramental grace, is a splendid gift from God to the spouses, and it is necessary if they are to live united to Christ in their married life. The baptized believer consecrates himself to the Lord in his union with his spouse and is enabled to make a religious offering of all aspects of his marital life. Marriage is necessary for the continuity and permanence of the family, since without it there would be a dangerous instability, the insecurity characteristic of transient unions, without permanent bonds that give support and a firm foundation to the life of the couple. Marriage is necessary in order to assure lifelong companionship, since "it is not good that the man should be alone", as Scripture says (Gen 2:18). The companionship of the beloved person over time is a permanent source of security and personal stability.

Furthermore, marriage is necessary for the religious and psychologically sound human education of the children. Certainly, in the modern world there are plenty of single mothers and fathers; nevertheless, it is certain that children need the presence of both parents, father and mother, for their appropriate, normal human development. The absence of one of them leaves a deep, cold void in the person's heart. For all these reasons and many more, Christian marriage is great and important: a holy sacrament, a sign of Christ's love for his Church; an indissoluble and monogamous union of husband and wife.

Union of man and woman

Precisely this idea of marriage as something exclusive between one man and one woman has recently been called into question by some. It is good to recall, however, that, according to traditional Christian moral teaching, sexual activity between persons of the same sex is unlawful and sinful. In this regard we have, among other reasons, the authoritative teaching of Scripture and especially of Saint Paul (Rom 1:24–27; 1 Cor 6:10). Thus the *Catechism of the Catholic Church* affirms and teaches it officially (*CCC* 2357–59).

Nevertheless, modern society is threatened by tendencies to promote homosexual relations indiscriminately and to establish, even legally, a stable union between homosexuals as a form of marriage. There is no doubt whatsoever that this definition does not apply to Christian marriage. However much we may give due respect to homosexual persons, this respect cannot lead us to consider that union as a true marriage.

OBSTACLES TO CHRISTIAN MARRIAGE

The *Synod Report* of the 2014 session clearly sets forth the greatness of marriage as a sacrament, as the basis for the education of persons, and as the foundation for the stability of the family (cf. nos. 12–22). Lamentably, these two institutions are not free from serious and severe threats in the modern world. It is important for us to look at several of these difficulties, especially the ones that may be encountered within the Church herself.

Cultural and economic obstacles

One of the chief threats or obstacles to marriage nowadays is secularism, which is increasingly aggressive in the Western world. Through the audiovisual and electronic media, through the Internet, the secularist tendency, or, rather, militant and specifically anti-Christian secularism, is becoming stronger and stronger. We are talking about the project to remove God and religion from social life and personal life and to relegate what is sacred, religious, and divine to the sphere of individual or private activity. The tendency to suppress or diminish expressions of religion is becoming ever stronger in Europe and some parts of America, especially in the cities, and, without any doubt, it undermines among today's young people the awareness of the value and importance of sacred things, religion, and Christianity. It would be naïve to ignore the fact that this secularizing tendency has imperceptibly contaminated some ecclesial circles.

Another obstacle to marriage, at least in Western culture and, lamentably, also in some ecclesial milieux, is superficiality and frivolousness about life, a culture of *the weak or fragile mind*, the law of the path of least resistance and the rejection of commitments. This is an attitude that shuns and rejects any effort, any demanding task, any need for lasting, continuous work. It is an attitude that favors convenience, personal preferences, and pleasure. And of course marriage, which requires commitment, fidelity, common work, stability, selflessness, generosity, effort to understand and support the other, to yield to the other in making decisions, does not come off well in this fragile mentality of contemporary culture.

Therefore, we find sexuality without commitment or love, free unions, temporary unions, cohabitation without a legal tie, much less a religious bond. This is a very big problem facing the Church in our time. It is necessary to confront it clearly and to make an effort to educate better the families and children and young people in our parishes and schools, so that they can overcome this complacent, soft, and easygoing mentality, which is incapable of anything that requires commitment, effort, or self-denial, in other words, the denial of one's tastes and preferences.

Economic problems, too, make marriage difficult. The difficult socioeconomic conditions of the modern world in most nations, including the most highly developed, such as unemployment, low wages, the scarcity and high cost of housing, also militate against marriage, since young engaged couples have problems establishing their own home.

Obstacles within the Church

Yet there are even more formidable obstacles. I mean chiefly the threat that weak education in the faith, combined with the secularizing milieu, poses for couples who are thinking of embarking on married life because they are simply not adequately prepared to confront in a spirit of faith and with a Christian view of life the difficulties of starting a new family.

Along these lines it is necessary to point out also that specifically evangelizing activity has grown cold in the pastoral care of many Christian communities. Therefore Pope Francis is constantly calling us to "go out" and communicate the gift of faith to our brothers and sisters. Recall that Paul VI, in his apostolic exhortation *Evangelii nuntiandi*, spoke to us about the explicit, public proclamation of the Lord's message (cf. 22, 26–29). Obviously, though, in some milieux we find instead a less active attitude, more timid and less explicit evangelization efforts than in other times, less constant work in educating the new generations in the faith. Secularism, which manifests itself, among other ways, in disrespectful attitudes toward the celebration of the liturgy, has something to do with this. Nevertheless, we should ask ourselves whether there has not been in many people a decline in the apostolic ardor typical of the great evangelizers, the dedicated pastors, and the Catholic educators of former days. Parishes where in the past seven or eight Masses were celebrated every Sunday now have three or four, if that many. There are Catholic schools where instruction in the faith is nil or weak, limited to a few hours per week, sometimes confused with "values education" and dispensing with the communication of the faith strictly speaking, that is, the instruction of children and youth in the splendid truth of Jesus. The result is that the general environment in which they live assigns little importance to religion and, therefore, to the reception and the celebration of Christian marriage.

We should point out also, although it is painful to do so, the weakness of catechesis and the pastoral care of young people in some places. There are parish communities where both programs are very much in decline or very weak. This is definitely a serious problem, since without it young people are deprived of the opportunity to come to know Christ and to participate in the life of the Church.

The proposal to admit the divorced and remarried to the Eucharist

Another new and very recent problem is the widespread proposal to admit—subject to several conditions, among them a period of penance—divorced and remarried persons to the table of the Eucharist. This hypothesis or scenario, already proposed many years ago, now has the laudable motivation of pastoral mercy that would seek to alleviate the spiritual suffering of those who have contracted a second civil marriage while an earlier sacramental marriage is still in force and, consequently, cannot presently receive Holy Communion. This proposal has met with much sympathy, since we all wish to be *merciful* and to mitigate the faults of our brethren.

Nevertheless, and with all due respect to its promoters, we maintain that this hypothesis, however well-intentioned it may be, contradicts the Lord's words in the Gospel as well as the teaching of Saint Paul (Rom 7:2–3; 1 Cor 7:10; Eph 5:31) and of the Church over the centuries. Specifically, it consigns to oblivion the still-fresh teachings of Saint John Paul II in his extraordinary and very relevant apostolic exhortation *Familiaris consortio* (1981). This document, published one year after the synod on the family in 1980, which the pope seriously pondered over the course of many months of study, reflection, and consultation, in communication with experts of various theological disciplines, clearly rules out this possibility (84).

The 1992 *Catechism of the Catholic Church* also reaffirms the traditional doctrine and the practice of the indissolubility of marriage, the conditions for going to Holy Communion, and the teachings of the Church about sexual morality:

> If the divorced are remarried civilly, they find themselves in a situation that objectively contravenes God's law. Consequently, they cannot receive Eucharistic Communion as long as this situation persists. For the same reason, they cannot exercise certain ecclesial responsibilities. Reconciliation through the sacrament of Penance can be granted only to those who have repented for having violated the sign of the covenant and of fidelity to Christ, and who are committed to living in complete continence. (*CCC* 1650)

Similarly, the *Letter to the Bishops of the Catholic Church concerning the Reception of Holy Communion by the Divorced and Remarried Members of the Faithful*, written in 1994 by the Congregation for the Doctrine of the Faith, reiterates the doctrine affirmed by the Holy Father in *Familiaris consortio*. More recently, in 2007, the Concluding Document of the Fifth General Conference of the Bishops of Latin America and the Caribbean in Aparecida, speaking about support for the family, asks us to "accompany with care, prudence, and compassionate love, following the guidelines of the magisterium, couples who live together out of wedlock, *bearing in mind that those who are divorced and remarried may not receive communion*" (437j, emphasis added).

We cannot contradict these teachings, nor can we forget the very recent teaching of Pope Benedict XVI in his apostolic exhortation *Sacramentum caritatis* (2007) on the Eucharist, which, citing the synod of bishops in 2005 on this august sacrament, tells us: "The Synod of Bishops confirmed the Church's practice, based on Sacred Scripture (cf. Mk 10:2–12), of not admitting the divorced and remarried to the sacraments, since their state and their condition of life objectively contradict the loving union of Christ and the Church signified and made present in the Eucharist" (29).

Given the insistence of those who cite the cultural changes in today's world as a reason for this new pastoral practice, it is necessary to recall that the negative conditions that affect the family and specifically marriage have been present for many, many years, and today they have merely made stronger the pressure of the worldly spirit, the spirit of evil, on the Christian community. The Church, however, cannot yield to the spirit of the world, to sin, or to the corruption of morals. On the contrary, united with Christ, who has overcome the world (cf. Jn 16:33), she is called to uphold the splendor of the truth even in the worst situations. The truth does not depend on acceptance by a majority. Neither does pastoral practice.

Furthermore, the new practice that would allow the admission of the divorced and remarried to Communion, after a period of penance but while continuing married life, would appear to overturn several elements of Church doctrine. Not only does it contradict the doctrine about the necessity and nature of ecclesiastical marriage, but it also renders it useless and superfluous; it denies the traditional doctrine about the conditions for going to Holy Communion, contradicting the words of Saint Paul: "Whoever, therefore, eats the bread or drinks the cup of the Lord in an unworthy manner will be guilty of profaning the body and blood of the Lord" (1 Cor 11:27). It also forgets the constant Catholic moral teaching about sexual activity, which is ordered to the conjugal love of husband and wife, which is licit only within sacramental marriage (*CCC* 2360–61). Finally, this novel hypothesis undermines the teaching about the soundness and veracity of the Church's Magisterium, which for centuries, allegedly, has taught an exaggerated, false doctrine that is contrary to the spiritual and moral good of the faithful. The Church, moved by the mercy of the Good Shepherd, will continue to seek ways to alleviate the pain of those who are in an irregular situation. But this hypothesis does not seem viable.

No doubt, the session of the synod to be held next October, in the light of revealed truth and with the eyes of mercy, is called to reflect with great clarity on the teaching of the Gospel and of the Church through the centuries about the nature and dignity of Christian marriage; about the greatness of the Eucharist and the necessity of being properly disposed for union with God in order to go to Holy Communion; about the necessity of repentance, contrition, and a firm purpose of amendment in order for the repentant sinner to be able to receive divine forgiveness; and about the firmness and continuity of both the dogmatic and the moral truth taught by the ordinary and extraordinary Magisterium of the Church.

Moreover, the synod will have to suggest courses of action that will strengthen marriage, make it more attractive to young people, and keep it alive in the hearts of spouses over time. In this way it will offer to Pope Francis very important means of promoting an intense evangelization of the family and a new appreciation of the sacrament of matrimony. Likewise, it will provide insights inspired by mercy that will more effectively help those who find themselves in irregular situations to alleviate their moral suffering and to practice their Catholic faith more fully. We should recall that even today divorced and remarried persons can draw near to the Lord, although imperfectly, by participating in the Eucharistic assembly, listening to the Word, praising the Lord, giving and receiving the sign of peace, and lifting up to Jesus their longings to be ever more closely united to him.

PASTORAL CARE AND PROMOTING CHRISTIAN MARRIAGE

Speaking of pastoral approaches, it is necessary to note that, for the Church, one of the most serious problems concerning Christian marriage and the family is the tendency of today's young people to do without a marriage contract and even to refuse to start a formal family as it has been known in recent centuries. They simply do not want to marry, or they want to postpone marriage for several years.

What is to be done, then, to reverse this trend or at least to present a positive, convincing message to our young Catholic men and women so that they might seek to marry and to start a family on firm, lasting foundations? This is the great challenge that we face, and of course the *Relatio synodi* of the extraordinary session of the synod outlined several points (cf. 20–44). Here we will simply make some concrete suggestions that have to do with the general pastoral ministry of the Church.

PASTORAL CARE BEFORE MARRIAGE

Ecclesial renewal: a renewed, evangelizing, enthusiastic ambiance at every level

It seems to me that before speaking about specific programs we need in the first place a stronger, deeper, and more joyful attitude toward the experience of Christian life on the part of the Church in general. Indeed, along the lines of the ecclesial renewal that Pope Francis is constantly demanding, I think that only a more deliberate, truly Paschal experience of union with God and of the joyous practice of the faith can influence young people in the midst of the secularized environment in which we are submerged, so that they might practice their faith and be open to the possibility of marriage as an enlivening encounter with Jesus Christ. But it is necessary for the members of the Church, especially for us bishops, priests, and members of institutes of consecrated life, to sense more deeply and to live more explicitly and openly our personal encounter with the Lord. We should really sense the joy of the Gospel, practice our faith without complications, and proclaim it without embellishments or false human respect. We must not allow ourselves to be contaminated by secularism and should forget about trying to be *modern* in a world that is anti-religious. Admirable examples in this respect are several new religious and lay institutes that, although they have been in existence for only a few years, have a great number of members, since they are filled with an intense spirit of faith, deep prayer, and generous, courageous apostolic action.

Speaking about spiritual renewal, in order to confront increasing secularization, especially in the Western world, the Church also needs to renew her awareness of her evangelizing mission and to strengthen her spirit and apostolic ardor, as Saint John Paul II insistently asked. This is something that we must beg from the Lord and promote in our rectories, religious communities, seminaries and houses of formation, and in the lay apostolic movements. This renewed awareness of apostolic mission will then make possible a clear, Paschal, enthusiastic, explicit proclamation of the name of Jesus and of his gifts for the world. This will lead to the revitalization of Christian communities, will lend greater intensity to the experience of the faith, and thus will promote the necessary ambiance so that young people will want to start their own family on the basis of an encounter with our Lord and united with him in their hearts.

Youth catechesis and pastoral care

Of course young people ought to receive their initial formation for marriage in their own families. But where family life is lacking or irregular or indifferent to religion, the parish has to step up, with catechesis and strong, solid pastoral programs for youth.

Then there is a need to intensify a systematic, attractive catechesis that will help young people to draw near to God, to become well acquainted with the fundamental truths of the faith, and to appreciate the values and the advantages of the family and of Christian marriage. This is a serious need, and the Church will have to make more of an effort than she does now to organize and provide catechesis that reaches the large majority of Catholic children and adolescents. On the other hand, it is necessary to devote time, energy, and both human and economic resources to work with young people. In these areas it seems to me that our debt to our young Catholics is past due.

Lay movements for the family apostolate

In Latin America in the 1960s a strong lay movement for the family apostolate began: the Christian Family Movement. This has been followed by others, such as Marriage Encounter, and so on. It is very important for dioceses and parishes to promote the participation and activity of lay people in these types of associations, which do great and successful work both in preparing young people and engaged couples for marriage and in supporting spouses in their married life.

Improving immediate preparation for marriage

We are faced with the major challenge (and sometimes we do not respond to it correctly) of offering to engaged couples a good immediate preparation for marriage. We are talking about premarital meetings or courses. These cannot be limited to one weekend. There ought to be meetings scheduled over the course of several weeks, so that the young people might deepen and appreciate their faith, reencounter the Lord, come to value the life of grace and the sacraments, and become well acquainted with the sacrament of matrimony and the requirements of Christian family life. For this purpose, we have to be able to rely on adequate facilities and with well-prepared, competent, and attractive facilitators. When all is said and done, great importance must be given to the knowledge and renewal of the faith on the part of engaged couples.

The sanctification of homes

One pastoral activity that bears much fruit, and therefore ought to be increased, is inviting couples who are cohabiting or married only civilly to celebrate a Church wedding. Many couples who at the time they started living together were not married in the Church, either for economic reasons or because of other circumstances, or even because they had a very weak faith and Christian life, usually respond very well to this invitation. Of course, it is necessary to propose this to them with a remedial catechesis that makes them see the sanctifying, transforming nature of the sacramental grace of matrimony. The celebration of such weddings, at special moments for the Christian community, especially when there are several of them, is usually a very beautiful event that has a multiplier effect in those communities.

PASTORAL CARE DURING MARRIED LIFE

Pastoral care during married life is another extremely important point that, lamentably, we are not addressing as conscientiously as we ought. We mean pastoral care to spouses, to the fathers and mothers of every family. For this ministry, it will be necessary to find support and to create facilities and programs that offer assistance.

Associations for the family apostolate

We have already mentioned associations for the family apostolate in the preceding section. These groups or movements are extremely valuable and accomplish tremendous work. I think that we should encourage them more, promote their growth and expansion, facilitate their formation, and supply them with support and guidance from priests, deacons, or religious, so that they can carry out effective work among parishioners, in parishes, and in other diocesan circles, as they normally do when they are well directed. This should be a fundamental element of the diocesan and parochial pastoral care of the family.

Preaching focused on the family and proclamation of the doctrine about marriage

One of the most straightforward means is Sunday preaching, which is certainly within our reach. Homilies can always or almost always contain references to family life, to family problems, as well as exhortations to the Christian renewal of the family. Likewise, it will be necessary to proclaim in the parishes at least once a year the doctrine of the faith about marriage, its nature and beauty, and the moral requirements of conjugal life. In this way any confusion about admitting persons who are in an irregular situation to Holy Communion will be cleared up.

Special meetings for families

One way to promote fidelity and family unity is to offer periodically special meetings for families. They can be held during Advent and the Christmas season, in Lent, on the occasion of Mother's Day and Father's Day; at the beginning of the school year, at the children's graduation, and so on. These meetings can have a character that is formative and at the same time festive, accompanied by some religious celebration. One example might be to organize a community meeting for couples who have been married for fifteen or twenty-five years, and so on. There could be special meetings for fathers or for mothers. Finally, these meetings and celebrations have the purpose of strengthening family life through prayer and the sacraments.

The celebration of anniversaries

Celebrations of anniversaries, for instance, silver or golden wedding anniversaries, are special moments for presenting a good catechesis and exalting the nature and beauty of marriage. It is an opportunity that must not be missed.

CONCLUSION

Under the influence of the Holy Spirit and with the docile reception of his inspirations, the synod session in October will be an opportunity for reflection by bishops from all parts of the world, along with experts, consultants, Christian families, and apostles of the family, gathered together as brethren and united with Pope Francis to promote the sanctity and welfare of the family in the world. The synod is not a mini-council, since it has no authority of its own, yet it has an important mission: to offer to the Holy Father reflections and proposals for the government of the Universal Church. We are sure that it will do that.

Beyond the polemics that the discussion of some theories may occasion, the synod should offer to the pope and to the Church, and to the world through him, a radiant, enthusiastic, and attractive view of

Christian marriage as the basis for a holy, united, pious, stable, and happy family. Moreover, it should make clearly delineated, concrete, feasible proposals for more energetic and effective pastoral action in relation to marriage and the family.

May the Holy Family grant us this grace!